STOP SELLING...
Start Clicking!

Ten Bold Steps to Boost Your Business through the Magic of Human Connection

FLO SCHELL, EdM

Copyright © 2006 by Flo Schell

All rights reserved. No part of this book may be reproduced in any form or by any electronic or mechanical means, including information storage and retrieval systems, without permission in writing from the publisher, except by a reviewer who may quote brief passages in a review.

ISBN: 978-0-9728940-8-1

Library of Congress Control Number: 2006933968

Printed in USA

Published by:

MP Press
A Division of
Femme Osage Publishing
1301 Colby Dr
Saint Peters, Missouri 63376

Author Photo by Keith Weller

Cover Design and Book Layout by Cyanotype Book Architects

Dedication

This book is dedicated to those special ones who have encouraged me, nourished me, given me chances, loved me, and made me laugh.
I am so grateful.

A Message from the Author

Dear Reader:

Congratulations! You're the owner of an independent or franchised business and you love what you do. But now you realize you have to be a salesperson, too! Much as you'd like your business to grow, you know it will not grow by itself. You're eagerly searching for a way of selling that is easy and comfortable for you.

Or, you're already involved in a sales career and yearning for a simple, step-by-step sales model with a fresh approach.

I wrote this book for you. I wrote it because I love selling and because I know that selling is an absolute necessity if you want to share your passions with the world.

I wrote it with the firm knowledge that you *already* have most of what it takes to use this system successfully. The rest is a simple, step-by-step process that you can learn, whether you're an introvert, an extrovert, or someone in between.

I wrote it because I have seen many skilled and competent professionals come to a halt with their business growth because they are so uncomfortable with the notion of selling.

And I wrote it because I know how hard it can be for those of you who are responsible for sales to motivate yourself, year after year, to continue to grow your business.

In 1993, even though I had no formal sales training, I was tapped to lead the Franchise Sales Department for Sylvan Learning Systems, Inc., the largest education company in North America. What I lacked in professional training was made up for in sheer enthusiasm. I felt a great excitement about how Sylvan Learning Centers could help kids!

So… new to the position and without a sales process in place…I was called upon to create one.

I asked myself, "If I were the customer making this buying decision, how would I want to be treated and what would I need to know?"

Based on my answers, I created a sales process that came from my best place… my heart.

Early on, I learned that if I "clicked" with an individual at the onset, we were likely to go the distance together. So I tried to create this "Magic Click!" with every prospect.

And guess what? It worked! Over a seven-year period, my sales team and I doubled the number of Sylvan Centers in the U.S. and Canada from 300 to 750+. We helped to bring Sylvan to its designation as the #1 Franchise Opportunity in North America.

I'm sure I wasn't born to be a salesperson. But I do know this to be true: I was born to excite other people about the things I believe in.

Welcome aboard! I am eager to share with you all that I know so that your businesses, too, will become wildly successful!

Here's to happy selling!

Warmly,

Flo Schell, EdM

Acknowledgements

This project has been a collaborative effort of the highest order. As with all projects, it has its own story. I cannot imagine the end result coming to such a healthy and happy conclusion without the many key people who have supported me in my life and in my work.

The writing of this book spanned a four-year period. It began when I was building my career as a new coach. It was during my coach training that I noticed how many wonderful coaches were struggling to build their businesses. These individuals were outstanding professionals, but uncertain about how to sell and market themselves and their services.

I was fortunate to come to my work as a coach with a strong background in sales. How could I use that good fortune to help my colleagues? I could write a book!

As my new career progressed, my business began to thrive. I became so busy keeping up with its growth that I had to put the book writing on hold. I continued, however, to learn new and innovative coaching skills to add to my repertoire.

This turned out to be a blessing. When I returned to the writing over the next two years, I was able to bring all of my new knowledge and a fresh perspective to the book. In other words, I was able to add evolutionary coaching principles to my already strong relationship-selling approach.

The result is a sales process that I love. It honors customers and is comfortable for business owners and sales professionals, too.

This process weaves in coaching skills such as deep listening and provocative questioning and eliminates the hierarchy that is prevalent in many sales experiences. It creates, instead, a selling and buying partnership that is built on collaboration and equality.

I am convinced that the profession of coaching and the profession of selling are perfect together!

And I've done all that I can to merge the two into a sales process that is caring and smart and a tribute to today's savvy customer.

As I embarked on this book-writing journey, there were so many teachers that appeared. Of course, my primary sources of nourishment were there from the start.

My mom, "Flo 1," who showed me how caring for others and selling could be successfully joined as one.

My dad, who reminds me from afar that real love never goes away.

My son Walt and his wife Kelly, who love one another joyfully, with a bit of whimsy and even big bold giggles.

My son Jeff, his wife Laura, and their precious daughter Ansley Joely, who demonstrate how a young family can grow strong together and create a thriving business, too.

My doggie René Stargazer, who provides me with irrepressible affection.

And my husband Charlie, who reminds me daily that intimate relationships are our #1 teacher. He has been my chief supporter for at least forever.

I am also fortunate to have a sister who makes great macaroni, a very chic brother-in-law, great cousins, and really good friends who make the weekends delicious and fun and a welcome respite from the work week. We spend a lot of time laughing around the dinner table. It doesn't get much better than that!

As my life and work changed in the mid-'80s, new mentors appeared. Bob Muir and Doug Becker gave me a chance to perform sales functions in the corporate setting. My love of sales was further enhanced by the personalities and comradeship of Tom Palazzo, Britt Schroeter, Pete Lorenzo, Kim Murdock, and Diana Whitman. Later, Scott Hurlock and Irene Vavas joined the team. We performed more like a family than a workgroup. Together, we surpassed 17 quarterly sales goals and had such fun! I am indebted to them all.

After 16 years in Corporate America, a very special teacher appeared. Maureen Simon, a California- and London-based Life Coach, helped me to experience the coaching model and inspired me to make it a part of my life.

It was she who introduced me to the work of Thomas Leonard, who I thank daily for creating the art of coaching. In my mind, he created this profession just in time for me!

As I progressed through coach training and early entrepreneurship, I received special guidance through the unlimited skills and talents of my own coaches, mentors, and role models.

How can I adequately thank Lisa Kramer, Terri Levine, Cheryl Richardson, the evolutionary managers and coaches at The Schools of Coachville, and Andrea J. Lee for offering me exactly what I needed at precisely the right moments? These thought-leaders and visionaries helped me to take off, soar, and eventually reach for the stars throughout each stage of my coaching career. Most important, they taught me that some of the best relationships in the world are created through the coaching process.

And I am first and forever grateful to all of my clients. They enter the coaching partnership with full faith and teach me much more than I could possibly teach them. I really treasure these individuals… their courage, their strength and their openness. They are truly growing into and living their best and most courageous lives!

Today, as we bring this particular project to completion, I am especially happy to thank these skilled and loving individuals who contributed in a vital way to its success:

- An enormous swell of gratitude to Andrea J. Lee, whose brilliance, light, and energy have enhanced my work in so many ways…

- A tribute to Eddy Goldberg, who saw me through at least two careers, for his extraordinary editing talents, his humor, and his loving nature…

- Huge bear hugs to my earliest and most respected pre-editors and readers: Walt Schell, Maribeth Pelly, and Mary Jo Kurtz for making those "oh-so-perfect" suggestions that brought me back to the drawing board…

- A big thank-you to Sarah Van Male, whose graphic arts skills are surpassed only by her patience…

- Big doses of gratitude to Lynne Klippel and Femme Osage Publishing for being there at just the right time.

- And a really special note of appreciation to the following respected individuals who served on my first R&D Team for this project: Lisa Kramer, Joan Pittenger, Eddy Goldberg, Mary Jo Kurtz, Bob and Jill Covey, Kathy Poehnert, and Jim Gober. Your input and encouragement got this book off the ground!

And a special and enormous thank-you to all of you who have chosen to read this book.

Congratulations! You are part of a heart-based movement that is sure to please the planet.

Table of Contents

Message from the Author … 5

Acknowledgements … 7

Definition:
The Magic Click! … 13

Helpful Guidelines for Readers … 15

Our Goal Together
Create the Best Sales Experience Ever … 23

The 3 Prerequisites
You Already Have Most of What It Takes … 33

PREPARATION STAGE

Step One
Know What Makes You Special … 43

Step Two
Choose Your Customers Well … 53

Step Three   67
Get Clear on Precisely What You Have to Offer

Step Four   73
Tell Your Customers How You Solve Their Problems

Step Five   81
Create a Marketing Image for Your Customers

Step Six   91
Reach Out to Your Favorite Customers

CONNECTION STAGE

Step Seven   101
Greet your Favorite Customers Everywhere!

Step Eight   115
Create The Magic Click! & Move the Relationship Forward!

Step Nine   131
Navigate the Land Mines & Come to Commitment

LIVING TOGETHER STAGE

Step Ten   149
Be Masterful with Your Customer Relations

Epilogue   163
When it's Time to Part… Create a Soft Landing and Stay in Touch for a Long, Long Time

Parting Words, Invitations, and Respected Resources   169

Are you Ready for Some Action?   171

About the Author   179

Definition: 'The Magic Click'

Think about the magical feeling of connection that sometimes occurs when you meet someone for the first time...

That 'spark' of curiosity that leaves you yearning to know more.

That 'spark'... that intangible moment of connection

is known as

The Magic Click!

Helpful Guidelines for Readers

*There are two types of language in the world: the language of the intellect and the language of the heart.
The language of the dry, rational intellect likes to argue and attack.
The language of the heart... is quite different.
Those who speak this language do not care about their ego.
They have no interest in proving they are right or that anyone else is wrong.
They are deeply concerned about their fellow beings.*
—AMMA, HUMANITARIAN

WELCOME ABOARD

Through the purchase of this book, you have taken the first step to creating a sales experience guaranteed to honor your own values and the values of your 21st-century customers.

Most important, this heart-based approach to selling will dramatically increase your comfort with the selling process, and thus your revenue and your bottom line.

This simple 10-step sales process is carefully crafted to combine the best of relationship selling skills with the best of today's evolutionary coaching principles.

It is certain to offer a new perspective on the compelling advantages available to you when the profession of coaching joins the art of relationship selling.

The process takes into consideration that today's savvy and informed customers want to *invite* business owners and sales professionals into their lives… rather than feel imposed upon by these individuals.

Whether you're brand new to selling or unhappy with the sales approach you're using now, wouldn't it be great to let go of any negative feelings you have about selling… forever?

I hope so, because you're in for a good ride!

The transition from the old kind of selling (where customers are sold through manipulation and pressure) to heart-based selling (where customers are sold through careful listening and problem-solving) is a process. It may even take some guts to apply. But it can be learned… and it is definitely a better way.

Ready? Here we go!

THREE PREREQUISITES

The Magic Click! is the hallmark of this sales process. It's about creating a connection that will ensure that your prospect will want to know you and your products and services better.

Three prerequisites will ensure that *The Magic Click!* works for you. With these in place, you will have all you need to create a sales process your customers will love!

1. The ability to live and work from your heart.
2. The facility to communicate cleanly and openly from your heart.
3. The capacity to create and maintain long-term relationships.

THREE STAGES, 10 STEPS
The sales process is divided into three stages:

1. Preparation Stage
2. Connection Stage
3. Living Together Stage

It also is divided into 10 steps (see the Table of Contents for an outline of these steps).

You'll find a majority of our time will be spent in the Preparation Stage. Great sales professionals know this stage is *most* responsible for a successful end result.

You'll also notice that each stage and step is clearly outlined for you. The objective is for you to get perfectly clear on how to prepare for your sales experience; how to connect and commit with your potential favorite customers; and how to grow your relationships over the long term.

THE HALLMARK OF THE PROCESS: THE MAGIC CLICK!
Your success with this process will be directly proportional to your ability to create a special feeling of connection with another individual.

Your prospects will come to you as virtual strangers. Your goal is to transition them into long-term customers.

Your ability to transform a brand-new meeting with a prospect into an ongoing partnership requires some special skills.

- First, you'll want to create a comfortable and easy conversation with this person that allows for impromptu diversion and a bit of fun.

- Next, you'll want to come from a place of curiosity and be eager to learn as much as you can about this new individual.

- And third, you'll want to listen more than you speak… for commonalities you share with this person… for similarities that can bring you together… for affinities that make you smile.

I have learned through the years that certain conversational connections are very special.

For example, while having an initial talk with a prospect you may discover that both of you grew up in the same town.

Or share a passion for the Dallas Cowboys.

Or get your favorite burgers at Foster's Grille.

As these conversational sparks occur, you feel a desire to learn more.

These sparks… these intangible moments of connection… these magic couplings… are the hallmark of my heart-based approach.

I call them *The Magic Clicks!*

When these fun connections occur, the sale is likely to go the distance!

Why? Because once you start having fun and sharing stories the relationship is bound to grow.

And once the relationship starts to grow, you will do all in your power to strengthen it and make it special.

And once the connection feels strong and special, no matter what roadblocks come up or what challenges you face, the relationship is likely to surmount anything.

This initial connection… this *Magic Click!*…is the beginning of it all.

CHOOSING THE WORD THAT MAKES THE MOST SENSE

Based on the type of business you're involved in, some of you work with "customers" while others of you work with "clients." While the definitions of these words are similar, they are not identical. For ease of reading I chose to use the word "customer" throughout this book.

Of course, until the "customer" becomes a part of your business family, he or she is really a "prospect." Truth be told, it seemed messy to be using the phrase "prospective customer" over and over again… so I stayed with the word "customer" in most cases.

So, whether you think of the individuals and organizations that you're courting as customers or clients or prospects, please substitute the word or phrase that makes the most sense for you.

Because whichever word you choose, our goal is one and the same… to convert those we're courting into real live actual customers!

When that happens, it's time to celebrate!

CREATING A WONDERFUL TEMPLATE

Each of the stages in this process is a building block for the next. Together, they form a wonderful template.

You will use the template to create an individualized sales process that is true to you.

The process is delivered in step-by-step order, but you get to choose how appropriate that is for you.

Depending on your reason for reading, you may prefer to start at the beginning, in the middle, or somewhere near the end.

INDEPENDENT BUSINESS OWNERS

If you own an independent business you will benefit from starting right at the beginning of this book and working your way through.

Many professionals, such as coaches, consultants, financial advisors, wellness practitioners, artists and technicians come to their business with outstanding skills and a keen interest in helping others. Often, however, they have little or no sales knowledge.

This book is perfect for all of you…no matter what your business!

FRANCHISE BUSINESS OWNERS

As a franchisee of a proven system, you are part of a unique and successful model for doing business. As an interdependent partner with your parent company, you will select the steps that reflect what you need, what you are responsible for, and what you can personalize.

Your parent company may have handled some of the steps for you. They may have researched the profile of your ideal customers, created initial marketing materials, and scripted your initial sales calls.

Still, I would suggest that you read the book in its entirety, build on the training delivered by your franchisor, and create a sales process that is authentic for you and compatible with your Franchise Agreement.

If you are a franchisee of a single unit, you will use this process to bring new customers into your business.

If you are an Area Developer or a Master Franchisee, you will find the process useful in attracting additional franchisees into your territory.

SALES PROFESSIONALS

If you're a new salesperson, I would suggest you start at the very beginning and work your way through. You'll know what to skim and what to pay close attention to based on your business.

As a seasoned salesperson, you might skip to Steps 8, 9, and 10 to find a time-tested approach to handling inquiries and beyond.

Whatever you choose, my wish is that the process will serve you and give you the confidence you need to be successful.

WHAT YOU'LL NEED IN ADDITION TO THIS BOOK

To keep all of your thoughts and ideas in one place, please purchase a Journal to accompany this book. Choose a color you love and a size big enough to contain all that you hope for.

You'll find a questionnaire in Step One. Then, each Step has an Action Plan at the end of the chapter. Please complete the full questionnaire and do the action items that call to you. Your answers and lists will have a home in your Journal.

CREATING A GREAT RESULT

At the conclusion of our time together, my big wish for you is this:

If you currently feel like a fish out of water in the world of sales, you will find yourself ready and eager to share the good news about your products and services with the world.

If you come already knowing plenty about sales, but feeling stale or bored or frustrated, you will leave feeling reenergized and open to trying on new perspectives and fresh approaches.

And, of course, you'll all be wildly successful!

I'm glad to have you aboard!

Our Goal Together: Create the Best Sales Experience Ever

> *The best and most beautiful things in the world cannot be seen or touched. They must be felt with the heart.*
> —HELEN KELLER

I think of this sales process as connection-based or heart-based... not in an effort to be syrupy, or even necessarily spiritual, but to emphasize that when we come from this place... this place called the heart... we come from our best place. We come from a place of authenticity, a place of openness, a place of integrity, and a place of genuine concern for ourselves and for others. Therefore we come from a place of ease. The sales process, when handled this way, becomes a natural way to communicate and create relationships with other people... and a way to help them get exactly what they need... not a way to convince them to do something they don't want to do.

Let's begin our work together by understanding what "selling" really is.

WHAT IS SELLING?

What is it about "selling" that has made it such a nasty word? Well, let's look at the definition. The dictionary defines the word "selling" in this way: to transfer property in exchange for money or something else of value.

Now, I ask you, "How bad is this?" And if not that bad, then where does the nasty connotation of the word come from?

Well, let's look at the definition again. Of all the words in the definition, which one brings up the most emotion for you?

My guess is that the word "money" is the one that shakes you up! Money is an extremely emotional issue for most of us, in varying degrees. We each have our own "baggage" about money. We each spend our money on different things and in different ways… and it's usually related to our own personal priorities.

But there are some ideas we do have in common about money. Most of us usually have a hard time "parting" with our money… particularly if we're unsure of the value we're receiving. And most of us want to get our "money's worth"… in other words, we want whatever we are buying to be a fair exchange for the money we are spending.

So *that's* what's really going on in the selling process. The customer is always weighing what they need with what it will cost them to get it… and deciding if that is a good and fair use of their money.

But there's something else going on here, too. The customer is also checking out the salesperson! They're asking, "Is this someone I want to invite into my life?"

Customers want to deal with someone they feel comfortable with and someone they trust. They've had experiences in the past with salespeople who have bullied them, or made them feel disempowered. So, they're asking, "Is this a person I want to buy from? Is this a person I want to let into my life?"

No wonder the sales process is intimidating to so many people!

And guess what this creates for you? It creates a wonderful opportunity… not only to change the way "customers" think about selling, but to change the way "you" think about selling, too!

A NEW DEFINITION OF SELLING

My heart-based approach to sales starts with a new definition of "selling"... a definition that helps us realize that selling is much more than a single event in which money changes hands.

In my definition of "selling," the sales experience is a process... a process that begins with solid preparation, moves into sincere connection, and plays out as a courteous way of living together with ongoing efforts to stay in touch.

Done effectively, the sales experience actually begins long before you ever talk to or lay eyes upon your prospective customer and it lasts long beyond the day your customer stops working with you.

So, may I offer you my personal definition? Here we go.

"Selling" is about:

- knowing what makes you special
- choosing your customers well
- getting clear on precisely what you have to offer
- figuring out your customers' problems
- communicating how you can solve your customers' problems
- creating an authentic image for your customers to see
- meeting and greeting potential customers
- creating *The Magic Click!* with each and every one of them
- moving the relationship forward
- coming to commitment and
- treating your customers well at every opportunity

in return for money or something else of value.

How does this sit with you? Is it something you're comfortable with? Do you see the words that have been added to bring more value to the exchange for money?

Together, the phrases of this definition form the basis of my heart-based approach to selling.

OUR GOAL TOGETHER: CREATE THE BEST SALES EXPERIENCE EVER

There is a wonderful food store in my town… chock-full of Italian delicacies… and none too inexpensive, either. The name of the store is Joe Leone's.

I'm a relatively new customer of Joe's, having just moved back to the area. Joe's a big guy… hard to miss… with a big smile… and on almost every occasion I've shopped there, Joe has personally said "Hello." Often he holds the door for his customers and even carries their bags to their cars.

On many occasions I have left Joe's with a stomach filled up with delicious food samples. Daily, Joe has his staff set out cheese, crackers, olives, and cookies. I snack away to the sounds of Frank Sinatra in the background. How happy can one be?

I have also learned that the higher prices I pay at Joe's are well worth the money. His food preparations are always fresh and delicious. On one occasion, I felt the need to return one food item that didn't taste quite right. Joe's response was to invite me to look around and choose whatever looked good that day. As I approached the register, with my new dinner and a few other items in my basket, Joe waved away my money, packed the bag himself, and walked me to my car. "I'm so sorry for the inconvenience," he said.

Now Joe Leone's is smack in the middle of a resort town, so traffic increases greatly on weekends and in summer. Sometimes the store is holding 30 or more customers at a time… in a small space.

But in winter and mid-week, things slow down a bit.

It was on a mid-week day that I made a visit to Joe's. I completed my shopping and was taking a look at the Italian rolls by the cash register.

I was about to order one when I saw a beautiful round loaf of bread that looked new and different to me. I asked about it and was told it was made with Asiago cheese and potato bread. Yum!

So I changed my mind and asked for that beautiful loaf instead.

Joanne, one of my favorite counter persons, smiled. She placed it in a bag and said, "Today this is courtesy of Joe. All he asks in return is that you tell us how you like it."

Well, I was amazed! How nice is this? I can't remember another time in my life when a shop owner just *gave* me something.

I was an absolutely delighted customer! And it wasn't lost on me that Joe was offering this surprise on a day when typically only "locals" were in the store. He would continue to win our hearts and our loyalty, something that would come in handy next summer when the lines got long and patience got short.

This, to me, is a selling experience that is smart and that comes directly from the heart! Most important, it does not represent a single orchestrated event… it is one of *many* heart-based experiences his shop offers.

The behaviors displayed by this owner and his staff absolutely fit my heart-based definition of "selling." Joe knows what makes his shop special. He knows exactly what type of customer he wants to attract. He knows what his customers want and need. He delivers exactly that. And when there's a problem, he goes beyond solving it. In essence, Joe is masterful with his customer relations.

Wouldn't it be great if we could create a sales experience for our customers that would leave them yearning for more?

OUR JOB TOGETHER

Our job together as we move through this book is to create a personalized sales process that will make both you and your customers smile… a process that is true to who you are and that allows you to come from your best place.

This process is akin to creating a long-term and special relationship… with all the qualities and characteristics that go along with that.

You will experience what it feels like to begin a sincere and open conversation with a brand-new person.

And you'll find that listening carefully, asking thoughtful questions, checking in to be sure you understand, and offering a considerate response are exactly what will make that person comfortable.

And once a comfortable beginning has been created, you will determine if what you have to offer is what that person needs.

Then you will have the opportunity to move the relationship forward and work together for a long, long time.

Here's what you'll know when we're through:

- You'll know exactly who you are.
- You'll be clear on precisely what you have to offer.
- You'll know exactly the types of customers that you want to attract.
- You'll learn where to find them,
- How to approach them,
- And what to say when you meet them.
- You'll learn how to take that initial meeting and turn it into a new relationship.
- You'll develop techniques for nurturing that new relationship into a long-term relationship based on trust and openness.
- You'll learn how to solve problems together.

- You'll know when it's time to say "good bye."
- And you'll know how to stay in touch for a long, long time.

All of this knowledge, put together, forms my Heart-Based Sales Process.

My pledge to you is that the work we do together will be worth the ride.

What will you pledge?

P.S.

I know that some of you may be feeling a bit nervous right now. You may know from experience how difficult it can be to attain sales goals. You may know that despite every good intention, there are times entrepreneurs or sales professionals may feel compelled to resort to persuasion techniques that are not in the customer's best interest.

So how, you're wondering, does that reality fit in with this process?

Well, the truth is this. There *will* be times when you will be challenged to meet high sales goals just to stay alive! There *will* be times when you will pull out all the tricks you know to move a prospect forward. And there *will* be times when your boss or wife or husband will be telling you, "*Just get the sale!*"

And you'll figure it out. You'll figure out how to be the best you can be… and get the sale, too.

Our work together is a work in progress. It doesn't happen overnight… give it time, be patient with yourself.

Our goal together is to attain sales quotas *and* to stay true to ourselves.

And we'll do that step by step and day by day.

Hang in there!

This Week's Action Plan
This week is about reframing our own thinking about "selling."

MOVING FORWARD FROM YOUR HEART

- Take a moment to purchase a new Journal this week. Choose a color that feels powerful and energizing. We'll call it *The Magic Click! Journal*. Keep it close by while using this book. It will be a useful tool as we move through the Exercises.

- Once you have your Journal, think of a sales experience in your own life that made you smile. What words would you use to describe the qualities, skills, and characteristics the salesperson used in this instance? How did the experience make you feel?

- Create a page in your Journal entitled, "A Great Sales Experience." Write the words that describe the experience on this page.

MOVING FORWARD FROM YOUR MIND

- Think of a sales experience in your own life that made you cringe. What words would you use to describe the tactics and qualities the salesperson used in this instance? How did this experience make you feel?

- Create a page in your Journal entitled, "A Poor Sales Experience." Write all the words and thoughts that come up for you on this page.

MOVING FORWARD FROM YOUR BODY

- Visit a store in your area this week. Watch the sales approach carefully. What makes you feel good? What makes you feel less than good? Would you return to this store again? Is there anything you'd like to share with the proprietor of this store?

MOVING FORWARD FROM YOUR SOUL

- If you could create a sales style that would make people smile and that would make people think highly of you… what components of that style would feel absolutely essential for you? How would you act? How would you speak? How would you present yourself?

- On a new page in your Journal, write about your "Ideal Sales Style."

The Three Prerequisites: You Already Have Most of What It Takes

> *If I only had a heart!*
> —THE TIN MAN, IN THE WIZARD OF OZ

So why would I think that you have most of what it takes… already… to sell successfully from your heart?

Well, obviously you already have a heart (that's the easy part!)

Your heart has helped you on innumerable occasions to understand the feelings of others and to communicate your own feelings. Your heart has helped you to move through difficult times in your relationships and to come out intact on the other end. Most important, your heart has allowed you to love, to nurture, to compromise, and to forgive… many, many times.

THE GOOD NEWS

There are just three prerequisites needed to benefit fully from my heart-based sales process. They are:

1. The ability to live and work from your heart.
2. The facility to communicate cleanly and openly from your heart.
3. The capacity to create and maintain long-term relationships.

As we proceed, you'll see that combining these prerequisites with the 10-step process is absolutely all that you need to be successful.

LIVE AND WORK FROM YOUR HEART

Let's think about the "way" in which you've lived your life up until today. I know there have been moments when you have lived and worked directly from your heart.

Let's take a moment to check it out. Will you gently place your hand on your heart… right now? Take a moment to feel it beating and keeping you alive.

As you think of what living and working from your heart might mean to you… what words come up? Write these words in your Journal now.

Did you come up with a list that looks like this?

- Empathy
- Compassion
- Honesty
- Caring
- Understanding
- Open
- Tolerant
- Trusting
- Giving
- Concerned
- Passionate
- Authentic
- Real

What other words would you add?

In truth, we are most effective in our lives and in our work when we are coming from a place of openness, empathy, and trust. Since our heart is our primary source of these qualities, we can concentrate on this place as we create new relationships in our lives… particularly with potential customers.

COMMUNICATE CLEANLY AND OPENLY FROM YOUR HEART

The second prerequisite is the ability to communicate cleanly and openly from your heart. What does it mean to communicate from your heart-space?

Imagine this scenario: You're having a conversation with a potential customer who is brand new to you. Imagine that they get to speak first and you just listen… without any response at all until they are completely through. As you listen, you try to "feel" what that person is saying… you try to "listen behind the words." Then, when they're completely finished, you speak to them from your very best place… from your heart. Perhaps you'll want to ask some questions to be sure you understand what they're saying. Or perhaps you'll simply want to acknowledge what they said with a few kind words.

Either way, I am sure this person will really feel heard.

This is what is meant by communicating from the heart. How special is this in our world? Usually we're so busy deciding what we're going to say back… that we're not even listening at all!

Communicating heart-to-heart means that we drop our masks. We drop the "faces" we've created to protect ourselves and just become "real."

When we listen and speak from our heart, we become adept at connecting with potential customers in a way that honors their needs. We listen more than we speak… at least until we are clear on our customer's needs. We ask clarifying questions to be sure we understand what's been said… and then we respond carefully in an effort to move the relationship forward.

In the sales process outlined here, we will intentionally use this type of communication with our customers.

CREATE AND MAINTAIN LONG-TERM RELATIONSHIPS

The third prerequisite is the capacity to start a new relationship and to maintain it over the long term.

Why? Because the process of selling from your heart is nothing more than making new connections and moving those connections forward into new relationships. Then it's about dealing honestly with the ups and downs of those relationships, nurturing them, and staying with them for a long, long time.

Think of just one relationship in your life that you would characterize as a "long-term" relationship… perhaps a relationship with a love partner, a spouse, a friend, or a favorite relative.

Can you remember the very beginning of that relationship?

What attracted you initially to that person? Was there an immediate physical attraction, or an attraction of the minds, or an indefinable mutual chemistry?

Can you think of some words that describe what it took, in the very beginning, to move that relationship forward from a mere beginning to an ongoing, real relationship? Write these words in your Journal now.

Does your list look anything like this?

- Attraction
- Desire
- Time spent together
- Open-mindedness
- Optimism
- Compatibility
- Common interests
- Communication
- Enjoyment

Now let's bring the relationship further along. Put yourself in the middle years of that relationship. Now you know each other really well, but life continued to bring surprises that challenged the relationship. You faced ups and downs with this person, even really tough situations that could have ended the relationship. And yet, you pulled through!

What words come to mind as you think of the qualities and characteristics that it took to keep this relationship alive… past the initial attraction phase?

Now your list may look something like this:

- Patience
- Understanding
- Communication
- Resilience
- Strength
- Forgiveness
- Compassion
- Compromise
- Self-examination

And now, place yourself in the relationship as it is today. What made it last this long, despite the ups and downs? What qualities and characteristics are you called upon to use every single day in order to maintain this relationship? What words come up for you now?

- Empathy
- Putting the relationship before your individual needs
- Negotiation
- Re-negotiation
- Sacrifice
- Give and take
- Faith
- Love
- Acceptance

- Loyalty
- Willingness to change
- Humility

Do these words sound accurate for you? What words would you add to this list? Or substitute? Write these words in your Journal now.

These are some of the qualities needed to create and maintain long-term relationships. I know that many of the qualities listed are ones you already have. I also know that you absolutely know how to do this part!

YOU ALREADY HAVE MOST OF WHAT YOU NEED

So, do you agree that living and working from your heart is something you already know? And that listening and speaking from your heart is something you already have experienced at one time or another? And that creating and forming long-term relationships is something you already know plenty about?

Then here's what I know for sure! Based on my own experience with "selling"… you already have most of what you need to sell successfully and directly from your heart. In fact, you are just about ready to go!

Why? Because you create sales relationships in the same way you create any meaningful relationships! You look for commonalities, you talk openly, you answer questions willingly, you speak with honesty and empathy, and you do everything in your power to move the relationship forward.

As for the rest, it is a learned, step-by-step sales process… a process you will be comfortable with, and a process that will "fit" who you are and how you want to be perceived.

I look forward to accompanying you on the journey!

This Week's Action Plan
This week is about paying close attention to your heart.

MOVING FORWARD FROM YOUR HEART
- Select a special someone in your life to "really listen to" this week. Let this person speak until they are finished. Then, respond directly from your heart. Note their reaction. How does this feel to you? Ask how it feels for them.

MOVING FORWARD FROM YOUR MIND
- Take a moment to look over all the word lists in this chapter. Are there certain qualities that are really strong for you? Create a column entitled "My Strengths" in your Journal and list them there. Now identify the ones that are a challenge for you. Place those in a column called "My Growing Edges."

MOVING FORWARD FROM YOUR BODY
- Check into your heart area this week. Close your eyes and place your hand on your heart. Feel the beating. Imagine that your heart area contains your Core Truths… the things you really value. Write down the core truths you find there. Can you incorporate these truths into your "Ideal Sales Style"?

MOVING FORWARD FROM YOUR SOUL
- Imagine your heart holds both joy and pain. First, take a quiet moment to be grateful for one of the joys you hold in your heart. Close your eyes and just picture that joy. Then, bring up one of the hurts

you are holding there. What will it take for you to release this hurt? Are you ready to let it go? Write in your Journal what it will take to make that happen. Consider taking one action step this week that will move you in the direction of letting it go for good!

PREPARATION STAGE

♡ Click

Step One: Know What Makes You Special

> *I am not afraid... I was born to do this*
> —**Joan of Arc**

Who are you and what were you put on this planet to do?

When I was five years old, I knew that one day I would be a teacher. Twenty-one years later, there I was... teaching 11-year-olds in my home town. Then, one day, I was asked by the principal to pilot a reading series. My charge was to use the series in my classroom, figure out what I liked and didn't like about it, and then present my findings to the other elementary teachers. This was fun!

Upon my leave-taking from that school, my fellow educators told me the only reason they adopted "my" reading series was because I "sold" it so well!

My next career had been born! Although it was many years before I was hired to actually "sell" anything, I did learn something immediately from that experience. I learned that when I believed in something and thought it was "the best," I would go to any lengths to convince others to believe in it, too.

PREPARATION STAGE

We are now ready to begin the Preparation Stage. It's about learning as much as you can about yourself and your prospective customers and using that knowledge to create an image and a sales style that will work for you!

TUNING IN

Is it true for you that there are things that you "just know" about yourself? Things like exactly which season of the year brings you the most energy?

And precisely what time of day is your strongest? And which day of the week makes you groan?

Once, in my early career years as a sales professional, I didn't have this knowing. So I struggled to make follow-up calls on Monday, even though that was my lowest-energy day. And I scheduled client meetings at 8:30 a.m., even though I was definitely not a morning person. I even forced myself to make 10 sales calls a day, whether I was "up" for them or not.

Oh, the lessons we learn!

As I matured, I learned to pay closer attention to my own body rhythms, to my own intuition, and to what made me shine and what made me cower. I was getting in touch with my own inner "knowing" and using it to my advantage.

That is my wish for you… that you really take the time to look inside and figure out what gives you energy and what makes you tick. And, conversely, that you figure out what makes you crazy and what grinds you to a halt.

And that you use this knowledge to plan everything… your life, your career, your weekly schedule, your vacations… everything!

And my promise to you is that the more you know yourself, and the more you honor that "knowing," the more balanced and stress-free your life and business will be.

And then you'll be ready to develop a sales process that is true to you and in sync with your real nature... and that allows you to work in a way that is effective for you.

So, how tuned in are you to your whole self? Have you thought about the qualities and characteristics that are unique to you? Can you describe yourself openly and tell others what makes you special? Shall we find out together?

I'm going to pose a series of questions to you... things for you to think about and write about. Your answers are the first step to really knowing yourself well. Take your time... this will take awhile. Answer each question as thoroughly as possible in your Journal. Give each question at least one full page... more if you wish. Have some fun with this... and we'll analyze your responses later.

Here we go.

(It looks long, and it is, but don't worry... it's the only one in the entire book!)

The Heart-Based Selling Questionnaire

Part I

Personality Type: Think about who you really are, without any pretense at all...

1. What adjectives would you use to describe yourself?
2. If your friends had to describe you, what adjectives would they use?
3. Do you consider yourself an introvert, extrovert, or a little bit of both?
4. Do you consider yourself a "high-energy" person, a "low energy" person, or somewhere in between?
5. Do you like to work alone or collaborate with others?
6. Do you really thrive on change, or do you like to stay put?
7. Are you a quick decision maker, or do you like to "ponder" before deciding? Do you prefer others to make decisions for you?
8. Do you schedule your day systematically, or "shoot from the hip"?

Part II

Areas of Strength: Think about a project, or a time, that led you to feel a huge sense of accomplishment...

1. Which of your qualities and skills made this project so successful?
2. What did bosses, co-workers, or clients say about you?
3. What was it about this project that made you shine?
4. If you had to choose the *one ability* that allowed you to succeed time after time after time in your life, what would it be?
5. What kinds of people help you to be your best?
6. What types of circumstances bring you high energy?
7. What is your most productive time of day?
8. What do you do better than almost anyone else?

Part III

Intuition and Internal Knowing: Think about the inner resources you have learned to count on to get you through the day or through a rough patch…

1. How does your body tell you to pay attention to something?
2. When your "gut" tells you something, do you listen?
3. Are those "gut" feelings usually right or wrong?
4. How would your life be different if you paid more attention to your "gut" feelings?
5. What does life feel like when you are connected with your inner knowing? Disconnected?
6. What can you do to trust your intuition more?
7. Do you participate in any quieting activities, like meditation or yoga… activities that are known to strengthen intuition?
8. If you had no one to rely on but yourself, where would you find your wisdom?

Part IV

Growing Edges: Think about the areas you wish to develop further… the ones that are not quite right, yet…

1. What does the "ideal you" look like… both personally and in your business?
2. If there is one action you could take, right now, to move closer to your ideal, what would it be?
3. Knowing that growth is forever, what area of your life or work do you want to focus on right now?
4. What situations feel threatening or intimidating to you?
5. What are the issues you tend to procrastinate about?
6. When you're operating out of fear, who can you go to for help?
7. What resources (people, books, etc.) can you identify that will allow you to "arrange" for self-confidence?
8. What new knowledge will bring you closer to your "ideal you"?

WHAT DID YOU LEARN?

So, how did you do? What did you learn about yourself? Let's try to sort out your answers.

Go back to your *Magic Click!* Journal.

Find the two columns you created in the previous chapter: "My Strengths" and "My Growing Edges."

Look at all of the strengths you identified through the "Selling from Your Heart Questionnaire." These may be positive personality traits, skills you've mastered, even a strong intuition you've honed. List as many words or phrases as you can in your "Strengths" column. (I hope you're smiling as you write them!)

Your "Strengths" column will consist of descriptive words that can be used many times over as you market yourself and your services. You'll see these words turn up in your voicemail message, your marketing materials, and even on your business card. Later, you'll even see them used in something called a "Care and Share." These are the words that describe the best of who you are and the best of how you work.

Now look at all of the "Growing Edges" you identified through the Questionnaire. These may be skills or bits of knowledge that you've yet to learn, personality traits that are getting in your way, or things that you fear and would like to overcome. List as many words or phrases as you can in that column. (Please be gentle with yourself here.)

This column will consist of words and phrases that point you in the direction of what you have *yet* to learn and what you have *yet* to strive for. They are the words that will point you in the direction of future training and learning.

Get the idea? In order for us to connect wisely with others, we must first be connected with ourselves.

In order for our customers to understand who they are "inviting into their lives"... we need to be clear about who we are. We need to know what makes us tick and what doesn't.

We need to acknowledge all of our gifts, strengths, and talents as well as those areas that are yet unperfected... our Growing Edges.

Our work together is about figuring out who we are, accepting ourselves for where we are right now, opening ourselves to new learning opportunities, and then growing into the best we can be. And then it's about capitalizing on our strengths and using them to sell ourselves and our services.

And finally, it's about putting one foot in front of the other and creating forward movement, each and every day, even when we're not sure where we're headed!

This Week's Action Plan

This week is about looking inward and learning about ourselves.

MOVING FORWARD FROM YOUR HEART

- Select two or three strengths to focus on this week. Use those strengths whenever you can as you move through your life. Don't be afraid to stand tall. These strengths are part of your best self.

MOVING FORWARD FROM YOUR MIND

- Select one "Growing Edge" to make progress on this week. Create an Action Plan to address this area, listing the actions you will take, the date the actions will be completed, and any resources you will need to accomplish the actions.

- Check in at the end of the week. How did you do? What is left to do? Transfer unfinished items to next week's Action Plan. Keep going, week by week, until you've addressed all of your "Growing Edges." I can't imagine a better plan for self-growth.

MOVING FORWARD FROM YOUR BODY

- Just "go with the flow" one day this week. See if you can step away from your usual routine and do some things differently. How does it feel to be free of your typical structure? Is there any part of your routine you'd like to change as a result?

MOVING FORWARD FROM YOUR SOUL

- What conclusions can you draw from the words you've placed in the Strengths column? How about the words in the Growing Edges column? What themes are coming up for you in each of those areas? Would you like to take any action steps based on what you've noticed?

Step Two: Choose Your Customers Well

Surround yourself with people, color, sounds, and work that nourish you.
—SARK

Imagine becoming acquainted with a person, an organization, or a company for the first time and feeling instantly attracted to them.

There is something about them that makes you want to know them better.

As you interact with each other, you seem to connect effortlessly.

You just know they could become one of your Favorite Customers... if they need what you and your business offer.

YOUR FAVORITE CUSTOMERS

I don't know of a businessperson or franchising organization in the world that hasn't selected a less-than-Favorite Customer at one time or another. Maybe they needed to build a solid customer base to get off the ground. Maybe they needed the money. Maybe their business could not stay afloat without five new customers that month. Whatever the case, they knew *up front* that this customer would be challenging for them, but they took them on anyway!

The truth is… this happens a lot… and while the experience might work out okay… it is typically less than optimal and may even be difficult. The end result can be unsatisfactory, too, and that's not so good for your reputation!

Consider how you might feel if you were a businessperson in a relationship with a customer that was wrong for you. You might feel anxious before each meeting. You might find yourself in a surly mood without even realizing why. As you meet with this customer, you might speak tentatively or guardedly. This might create a less-than-honest interchange. And finally, when the meeting is over, you might be left feeling ineffective and unsuccessful.

How much fun is this? Is it worth it?

The good news is that you get to choose!

You know who you're naturally attracted to and who you're not. And here's what I know for sure… it's a lot more fun, a lot more satisfying, and a lot more effective to work with people, organizations, and companies that you feel an affinity with.

Now, depending on the type of business you're in, your Favorite Customers may be individual persons, organizations, or companies… or some combination of these.

So let's look at all of these possibilities as we begin to identify your Favorite Customers!

ATTRACTION AND HARMONY

We're attracted to people, and even organizations and companies, for so many reasons. Perhaps they "mirror" us in some way, remind us of ourselves. Or maybe they stand for something that we admire, or possess qualities we wish we had.

Because of these reasons, we may feel drawn to them… like we're being pulled in. Or we may feel an instant kinship with them… as if they were family. You know the feeling… the feeling that this is a person or organization you would like to know better!

Wouldn't it be great if this person, organization, or company that is so attractive to you could be harmonious with you as well?

Harmony comes about when two or more people create a pleasing combination together. They easily adapt to each other's styles, solve problems together smoothly, and are at their very best with one another!

A harmonious relationship is exactly the type of relationship that you want with a prospective customer… right?

Right!

And when the relationship is coupled with attraction, the chances of it going the distance are likely.

Does this mean you'll never work with a person, organization, or company that is unattractive to you, or that you don't feel harmonious with? Probably not! But then again, that's your choice! You get to decide!

YOUR FAVORITE PEOPLE, ORGANIZATIONS, AND COMPANIES

You are already connecting with people, organizations, and companies in your life that you totally enjoy! When you're with them you feel comfortable, or stimulated… even happy!

They may intrigue you or delight you. You may find them interesting… even brilliant.

Let's conjure up a few.

YOUR FAVORITE PEOPLE
We'll start with the favorite people in your life.

For a moment, just close your eyes and picture a blank movie screen appearing right in front of your eyes. Now go ahead and place one of your favorite people on this screen… someone you enjoy, look forward to being with, and have a thriving relationship with.

Now, take a really good look at them… scan them from top to bottom. What is it about this person, outwardly, that attracts you? What does their overall look say about them?

Now look at this person in a new way… look at them as someone you have come to like and admire for more than their outward appearance. Notice that there is a whole and vital human being inside of that outward shell… with thoughts and ideas and ways of speaking, listening, and acting that you admire.

What are the inner qualities you admire about this person? What do you like about the way they think? What do you like about the way they communicate? What do you like about the way they treat you?

Open your eyes and re-enter the world. When you're ready to begin, open to a fresh page in your Journal. Write this person's name at the top of the page. Now list every trait, attribute, characteristic, and quality this person possesses that you enjoy or respect. You can use words, phrases, and sentences to do this.

Perhaps your page looks like this:

Sophie Wilkins
- Easy-going
- Interested in trying new things
- Communicative
- Kind-hearted
- Open-minded

- Likes challenges
- Financially able

Now let's think of a second person you feel drawn to… and let's place their image on a new blank movie screen.

Go ahead and close your eyes again and bring them right up.

Scan them from top to bottom in the same way you did before. Notice all that you enjoy about their appearance. Then look inside and discover their core goodness… the way they think, the way they speak, and the way they act.

Honor them with a fresh, new page in your Journal. Go ahead and list their name at the top and write away. Maybe your second entry looks like this:

Todd Rose
- Ambitious
- Confident
- Competitive
- Fun to be around
- Great sense of humor

Now let's add another, then as many as you wish.

Kelly Worth
- Energetic
- Searching
- Ready for change
- Looking for guidance
- Shy
- Good person

Okay, now you've got the idea! Keep this going until you've listed all of your very favorite people… all the people who help you feel good about yourself and who help you to thrive!

YOUR FAVORITE ORGANIZATIONS

Now let's do the same with the organizations and companies you feel great about. After all, if you're in the business-to-business sector, your business will be marketing itself to other organizations and businesses.

Perhaps you'll think of a department store that has great prices, your favorite line of clothing, and really helpful salespeople… a grocery store that carries all of your favorite foods… or an online company that serves your personal and professional needs.

Go ahead and place the organization or company name at the top of a fresh page in your Journal. Now begin to list all the qualities and characteristics of this organization that you like, respect, and admire.

Your first listing might look like this:

Joe Leone's Food Store
- Courteous
- Generous
- Consistent
- Customer-oriented
- Values me
- Friendly
- Goes overboard to please
- Great food

Now do the same for at least four other organizations or companies that you absolutely enjoy dealing with.

Some of your listings might look like this:

Trader Joe's Market
- Great ambiance
- Good quality products at lower prices
- Friendly checkout people
- Carries foods I like
- Products are well displayed
- Great food samples
- Upbeat

Amazon.com
- Easy to access
- Lots of merchandise
- Safe credit card transactions
- Partners with other companies for hard-to-find items
- Free shipping
- Offers me selections based on my sales history
- Personalizes my experience

You've got the idea!

WHY SHOULD YOU TAKE THE TIME TO DO THIS?
The work you do in identifying your Favorite Customers will illustrate to you the natures of the people, organizations, and companies that you relate to best and wish to attract as customers.

We'll define your Favorite Customers as those customer types you click with, are attracted to, and are harmonious with.

Your job now is to seek those very same qualities and characteristics in the people who actually *need* your products and services.

YOUR IDEAL CUSTOMER PROFILES
Now that you've gotten clear on the types of customers you prefer, you'll want

to match them up with the types of customers you *need*. In other words, the customer types you want to attract must also be part of your target market.

Your target market is defined as those customer types you are marketing to and that you see as being perfect candidates for your business offerings.

If you are a consultant in the corporate world, your ideal customers may be CEOs of Fortune 500 companies or middle managers of IT companies.

If you are a wellness practitioner specializing in stress reduction, your ideal customers may be exactly this same group of individuals.

Your ideal customer is a compilation of all the qualities and characteristics you have identified as being perfect for your business offering.

Most businesses have more than one Ideal Customer Profile and identify a number of customer profiles suited to their business.

A FEW IDEAL CUSTOMER PROFILES

In my franchise coaching and consulting business, I have three or more Ideal Customer Profiles. Here are a few of them by title and with some of the qualities I'm seeking:

CEOs whose companies use franchising as a business model
- Open to new perspectives
- Seeking quality consultants to assist with change
- Sees outsourcing as a way to bring in fresh ideas

Sales managers of franchise companies
- Faced with a large sales goal
- Looking for new ideas
- Wanting a review of their sales process

Sales professionals in franchise companies
- Seeking growth, ambitious
- Frustrated, ready to learn a new model of selling

- Eager to receive ongoing training

My goal, always, is to find Ideal Customers who have as many of the characteristics of my Favorite Customer types as possible.

Then I'm a happy camper!

YOUR NEXT STEP
Go to your Journal and list every quality and characteristic you are seeking in your Ideal Customers.

This is the first step in identifying what you're looking for in your target market.

After this initial list is created, you'll be creating *several* Ideal Customer Profiles. This process will help you see there is more than one Ideal Customer type for your business.

If you are a chiropractor, your first list might show that you're seeking individuals who are:

- In pain
- Searching for relief
- Open to a new method
- Covered by insurance or able to afford treatment
- Willing to stick with the program until better

If you are the owner of an independent senior caretaking facility, your first list might describe individuals who:

- Are 65 years or older
- Meet criteria for Medicare
- Are able to function independently
- Require minimal assistance

Now it's your turn to create as many Ideal Customer Profiles as you can for *your* business. Write those profiles in your Journal and give them a name.

Our chiropractor might have profiles with names like these:

- The Aching Back
- The Need to Relax
- The Chronic Pain
- The Sudden Injury

At this point, the goal is clear. You want to select Ideal Customers who have as many of the characteristics of your Favorite Customers as possible.

Then you'll be happy campers, too!

THE SECRET

The secret here is to be very concise about what you like about your Favorite Customers… and just as concise about the qualities you're listing in your Ideal Customer Profile.

Then, your job is to begin looking for these types wherever you go.

Now keep in mind that it might not be possible to attract the whole enchilada in every case, but at least you know what works best for you!

The more clarity you have about the *types* of customers you seek, the easier it will be to find them… and then to market to them.

At this juncture, the more Favorite Customer types and the more Ideal Customer Profiles you can identify, the better. Then you'll have plenty of types to seek out.

Because here's what I know to be true… when you work with customers that are well-suited to your personality, you can talk and listen in a way that feels effortless!

You can get over humps with them, solve issues together, and smoothly negotiate rough patches.

What I'm saying is… you can come from your best place… directly from your heart!

CHOOSING LESS-THAN-FAVORITE CUSTOMERS

Often brand-new businesspeople feel compelled to take on customers they know are not a perfect fit. The goal is to create a base of customers to keep the business alive.

While this is not optimal, it may feel necessary. So let's pose a challenge that will make this more interesting.

Wouldn't it be great if you could use all of your heart-based people skills to transform a less-than-Favorite Customer into a Favorite Customer?

Here are a few examples:

- **The Customer:** You take on a customer that tends to communicate through anger. You had a hint of this in the get-acquainted process, but you went ahead anyway.
- **The Heart-Based Approach:** Rather than becoming defensive or arguing back, you listen carefully and acknowledge the customer's anger. Together you come to a solution.

- **The Customer:** Your less-than-Favorite Customer is consistently delinquent in their payments.
- **The Heart-Based Approach:** Rather than holding your anger in or choosing to live with it, you ask, "Is there anything I can do to make the payment schedule easier for you? Would payment by credit card solve your problem?"

- **The Customer:** This individual always arrives late for appointments. They were late the first time they met you!
- **The Heart-Based Approach:** Rather than fuming inside and feeling

disrespected, you ask what's going on. You come from a place of curiosity. Perhaps the time slot is troublesome for them. Perhaps there is ambivalence about coming at all. In any case, an open conversation will allow you to find out and bring the issue forward.

- **The Customer:** You take a person into your business or franchise system that doesn't fit your Ideal Customer Profile, but you need the sale. Your business model requires customers willing to put 100 percent effort into getting the desired results. This customer has other obligations that take up 50 percent of their time.
- **The Heart-Based Approach:** You have an open talk with this customer. You tell them you believe their desire to succeed is genuine. You brainstorm ways to put the other obligations aside over a three-month period. The compromise? At the end of 90 days, they will be ready to put 100 percent effort into the business . You put that expectation in writing.

If you feel obliged to accept less-than-Favorite Customers consider this: you can do your best to use all of your heart-based skills and turn this customer around... right into the type you enjoy and need best!

Now that's a challenge I like!

This Week's Action Plan
This week is about observing who you enjoy connecting with and why.

MOVING FORWARD FROM YOUR HEART
- Create an actual "Prospective Favorite Customers List" this week… people, organizations, and companies you *already know* who may need your product and services. These are real prospects with the qualities and characteristics you enjoy and admire… and with whom you think you will be harmonious.

- List them from A-Z in your Journal, leaving plenty of space for each letter. You will add to this list continually as you think of new entries. These people, organizations, or companies don't need to *be* just like you, *think* just like you, or *act* just like you… you simply need to enjoy them!

MOVING FORWARD FROM YOUR MIND
- Ask yourself what *types* of people, organizations, or companies you are most attracted to. Which of these *types* may need your product or service? Can you give these types a name? For example; Busy Professionals, Home Owners, Newlywed Couples, Nature Lovers, Soccer Moms? Add the names you've given to your Favorite Customer Types to your Journal.

MOVING FORWARD FROM YOUR BODY
- Actively get moving this week… get out and invite one of your favorite people to lunch. Or schedule a meeting with one of your favorite organizations or companies. Really notice all of the qualities that make them a *favorite* for you.

- When you come home, add these qualities to your list.

MOVING FORWARD FROM YOUR SOUL

- Be open this week to discovering the best in everyone you meet. Sometimes it's refreshing to get to know people, organizations, and companies that are *not* like you! They offer new perspectives and new ways of looking at life.

- As you observe them, notice what makes them unique. Look for their brilliance. Looking for the good in others… even those different from yourself… may add to your own openness and may offer a few surprises! So, smile and keep an open mind. What do you have to gain? Only a few new Favorite Customer Types!

Step Three: Get Clear on Precisely What You Have to Offer

> *You do not merely want to be considered just the best of the best;*
> *you want to be the only ones who do what you do*
> —JERRY GARCIA

You now know that you have any number of Favorite Customers out there just waiting for your product or service. These people, organizations, and companies are your target markets. This next step is about getting clear on the problems you solve for your target markets.

YOUR OFFERINGS ARE DIRECTLY RELATED TO YOUR CUSTOMERS' PROBLEMS

We all have problems! Your Favorite Customers are no different. Wouldn't it be great if your business offerings could solve the exact problems your prospective Favorite Customers face? Isn't that what all customers want… to have their problems solved?

If your customers are typical of most 21st-century humans… they're feeling overwhelmed, frustrated, and isolated… all by-products of The Information Age!

They're also faced with the daily issues of life… people issues, time issues, and money issues.

Peoples' lives are busy and complex. Almost everyone needs some extra help managing the feelings and issues that arise from intense lives, economic challenges, and fast-paced work.

Whatever your business, whatever your products or services, it will fare best if it clearly meets the needs of the people or organizations who will actually use them.

And it will really thrive if it solves their problems!

When you are describing your business to a prospective customer, your job is to let people know… clearly… what you can do to help.

Your job is to solve their problems.

PROBLEMS AROUND OVERWHELM, FRUSTRATION, AND ISOLATION

We live in a time that has us universally feeling challenged by too much to do and not enough time or help to do it.

The thrust of today's life puts most of us in a perpetual state of motion. We have so much to attend to… work and families… babies and parents… friends and siblings. We have groceries to buy, contracts to write, dinners to make, work to attend to, e-mails to answer, soccer games to go to, and bills to pay.

All within 24 hours a day!

Overwhelm can occur when we start making decisions on auto-pilot. When we make our daily choices this way, we forget to tap in and find out how our bodies and souls feel about each choice. Is it any surprise we feel overworked, underappreciated, and absolutely exhausted?

In former generations, our ancestors came together and chipped in during times of overwhelm. They gathered round when a new baby was being born and when a friend was sick.

Today's humans are often going it alone. Relatives and friends are geographically dispersed. Single women and men find it hard to meet a life partner of choice, and choose to live their "best lives" alone. Many people work from home, without benefit of colleagues and socialization. Our senior population is living longer than ever… often outliving their spouses, friends, and family members.

No wonder we feel isolated. No wonder we feel tired. No wonder we feel anxious. We are trying to control and handle everything on our own!

Our feelings of isolation contribute to our feelings of overwhelm, which contribute to our feelings of frustration. Is it any surprise that many of us feel disconnected… from ourselves, from one another, perhaps even from a higher source?

What is the result? We've become a planet of humans moving forward at top speed… and winding up tired, unbalanced, lonely, and stressed!

So ask, "What can you and your business do to help these humans?"

PROBLEMS AROUND PEOPLE, TIME, AND MONEY

There also are the typical, yet emotional, problems that beset all of us in our daily lives. They are the problems we experience around people, time, and money.

Imagine if your business had solutions to the problems we all have around the people in our lives… things like:

- How can we be in relationship, yet maintain our independence, too?
- How can we communicate more clearly with the people we care about?
- How can we solve problems with the people we love?
- How can we handle competition with the people we work with?
- How can we deal with difficult people and situations?

Now imagine if your business had solutions to the problems we all have around time (and lack of it)… things like:

- How can we manage our families and work and find time for ourselves, too?
- How can we prioritize our days so that the most important things get accomplished?
- How can we do our tasks joyfully instead of rushing through them?
- How can we manage our lives so that we can eat well?
- How can we use technology to save us time rather than give us more work?

And finally, imagine if your business had solutions to the problems we all have around money… things like:

- How can we create a budget and stick to it?
- How can we best invest our money?
- What is the safest way to get out of debt?
- Where is the best place to get a low-interest loan?
- How can I monitor my expenses better?

OUR PROBLEMS ARE UNIVERSAL

Most of us on this planet today have the same problems. Many individuals are carrying more than one job… even supporting more than one family. Add to that an economy that is continually shifting and retirement plans less certain. The result… our Baby Boomers will be working for a long, long time.

Even the really smart people of the world have trouble figuring out the financial side of life. This is a skill that can be learned, but many of us don't have the time or the desire to learn it. So we put our money into the hands of others, or we keep it safe in our local bank. Each quarter, we hold our breath and hope we're solvent.

People are yearning for help with their issues around overwhelm, frustration, isolation, people, time, and money. And they're yearning for reputable providers and organizations that can offer that help with integrity, knowledge, and cost-effectiveness.

Are you that provider or organization?

This Week's Action Plan
This week is about knowing how you can help yourself and others to solve problems.

MOVING FORWARD FROM YOUR HEART
- Put yourself in the place of one of the closest persons in your life. It could be your husband, wife, or significant other. It could be your child, your parent, a friend, a boss, or a colleague. Write their name on the top of a new page in your *Journal*. Now list every problem you think this person may have. Does this give you greater empathy toward this person? Do you see them in a new way? Is there anything you can do to help them solve a problem or two?

MOVING FORWARD FROM YOUR MIND
- Research shows that successful people take the word "problem" and replace it with the word "opportunity." If you're already there, congratulations! If you're not there yet, you might want to incorporate this new way of thinking and speaking into your communication style. As you start speaking differently, notice any changes in the way you and others react.

MOVING FORWARD FROM YOUR BODY
- We often hold our "problems" in our bodies. Next time you experience a problem, close your eyes and try to identify where you are feeling it in your body. Is it in your belly, your neck, or your head? Some other place? What does it feel like? Is it swirling around? Is it tight and solid… or tingling and nervous? Now put your attention right on that place in your body. Try sending some good deep breaths right there. When you feel ready, open your eyes. Just notice how the "problem" feels now. Any different?

MOVING FORWARD FROM YOUR SOUL

- Once I had the good fortune of attending a weekend training session conducted by nationally renowned coach, Cheryl Richardson. At the end of the seminar someone asked, "What can I do right now to be the best coach I can be?"

- Cheryl's reply, to the best of my recollection, was this: Go home and look at your life. Figure out what's not working…and what is a problem for you. Then…do all that you can to fix those things! That's what will make you a great coach!

- What can you do, right away, to fix the problems of your life? Wouldn't it be great to be the best person you could be?

Step Four:
Tell Your Customers How You Solve Their Problems

> *If you give something worth paying for, they'll pay.*
> —Thomas J. Peters

It's time to tell the world what you do!

After all, you're great at what you do... and becoming greater every day.

You've received more than adequate training and are invested in lifelong learning. You have created a fee structure and product pricing that is fair and competitive. You've taken the time to figure out what makes you special and unique. Yet, sometimes you feel tongue-tied when someone asks you what you do.

My wish for you is that you'll never feel tongue-tied about this again.

Are you in?

SO, WHAT IS IT THAT YOU DO?

Let's review the products and services you offer and how they can solve the problems of your Favorite Customers.

We'll start with the universal problems we've already identified... the problems of overwhelm, frustration, isolation, people, time, and money.

What do *you* offer that can help people in these areas?

Turn to a fresh page in your *Magic Click!* Journal.

At the very top of the page, place these words: "What I do to help my Favorite Customers with overwhelm."

On this page, with your Favorite Customers in mind, begin listing all the things you or your organization can do to solve the problems of your Favorite Customers around the issue of overwhelm. Be as specific as you can. Keep writing until you've noted every single thing you can think of.

When you've used up all your ideas, begin a new page. On this page place the words, "What I do to help my Favorite Customers with frustration." Now list all the things you can offer around that topic.

You'll continue in this fashion until you've completed all six of the universal problem areas we've identified. Keep your pen going until you've listed every single thing you can offer that solves problems for your Favorite Customers in the areas of overwhelm, frustration, isolation, people, time, and money.

If you run out of ideas, tap into your network. Ask someone close to you what you might have missed. Keep writing until your pen runs dry. In this case, the more problems you find, the merrier it gets.

SAMPLE JOURNAL SHEETS

In my role as a Personal and Business Coach, my Favorite Customers are individuals who are open to personal growth, who are actively seeking to make positive changes in their life, and who are ready and willing to do the work that will bring them there. Samples of my journal entries might look something like this:

What I do to help my Favorite Customers with overwhelm
- I help people identify those things that matter most to them… so they can prioritize better.

- I help clients reduce unnecessary tasks by suggesting they track daily activities for one week and notice what could have been eliminated.
- I help clients redesign their environment so they can accomplish more, but in an easier way.
- I suggest that clients "put themselves first" for one week… and see what they notice.

What I do to help my Favorite Customers with frustration
- I teach clients stress-reducing techniques.
- I introduce clients to an exercise called "The Wheel of Life Balance," which helps them visualize the areas of their life that are feeling satisfactory and those that are not.
- I talk with clients about the necessity of self-care and show them how to schedule nurturing activities into their daily calendar pages.
- I offer "In the Moment" coaching calls when a client is having a bad day.

What I do to help my Favorite Customers with isolation
- I suggest home-based clients seek alternative work spaces, such as going twice a week to a local Internet cafe.
- I ask clients to consider scheduling daily calls with a colleague, just to keep in touch.
- I introduce clients to the idea of a "buddy system." This is someone they can check in with weekly to review accomplishments and progress.
- I suggest clients schedule work dates outside their office.

What I do to help my Favorite Customers with people
- I help clients explore what is getting in the way of their relationships.
- I introduce clients to Heart-Based Communication.
- I help clients come up with alternate ways of problem solving.
- I offer clients a fresh perspective when they're feeling stuck about a particular people problem.

What I do to help my Favorite Customers with time
- I help clients identify and prioritize the things that are important to them.
- I teach goal-setting and prioritizing.
- I help clients create "fail-safe environments" that will support their life and work.
- I help clients get their toughest task out of the way by suggesting the concept of "swallowing the biggest frog first."

What I do to help my Favorite Customers with money
- I invite clients to talk openly about their money issues.
- I offer options on ways clients can earn supplemental income.
- I assist in finding an appropriate financial planner.
- I provide marketing guidance designed to build their business.

You get the picture! People everywhere are yearning for products and services to help them solve their problems.

Your Favorite Customers are looking for someone who will solve their problems, too! So, whoever *you* are… *you* are in business for the sole purpose of solving the problems of your Favorite Customers.

TELLING PEOPLE WHAT YOU DO
When someone asks me what I do for my living, I answer by telling them about the problems I solve.

For example, in my role as a Professional Life Coach, I might say this: "I work with people and companies that are looking to make a positive change in their life or work and want some support around that."

Or, in my role as a Business Coach, I might say this: "I help owners of small businesses find their unique selling voice."

Or, in my role as a Franchise Sales Coach, I might say: "I help companies that use franchising as a model, like Curves or Dunkin' Donuts, to grow their businesses."

Or, "I help franchise salespeople grow their revenue and their job satisfaction."

What will *you* tell people?

If you are the owner of an interior design business, your job might be to help people solve their problem of not knowing how to create the look they want... or not knowing how to do it on the budget they have.

When asked what you do, you might say: "I solve space problems for my clients within their budget."

Or you might say: "I partner with families who want a beautiful and functional space, but don't have the time to create it."

If you are the owner of a financial services business or work as a financial salesperson, you might say: "I save my clients a lot of time by going through the maze of investment options for them."

Or you might say: "I provide solid financial solutions for you, no matter what your risk level."

If you are the owner of a wellness studio or a spa, you might say: "I melt away your problems in a single session."

Or, "I help your body to relax so your mind can relax, too."

So, put yourself in *your* prospective customer's life. What problems are they facing on a day-to-day basis? And what can you say that will explain how *you* can solve them?

This Week's Action Plan
This week is about communicating clearly and concisely which problems you solve and how you do that

MOVING FORWARD FROM YOUR HEART
- In your Journal you listed all of the ways you help your Favorite Customers in the areas of overwhelm, frustration, isolation, people, time, and money.

    These are your Unique Solutions to your customers' problems.

- Now choose those Unique Solutions you like best. Write your solutions in sentence form, as in: "I help families keep their money as safe as possible in a volatile market."

    Once you've got a handful of favorites… practice saying them over and over… until the words become a part of you!

    Because these favorites, my friend, will answer the question: *"What do you do?"*

MOVING FORWARD FROM YOUR MIND
- Today we don't earn our customer's trust by trying to sell them something they don't want or need. Instead, we earn their trust by asking them, "What can I do to make your job (or life) easier?"

- What are some other questions you can use to find out what they need? Note them in your *Journal*.

MOVING FORWARD FROM YOUR BODY

- The old sales model was about convincing someone they needed what you were selling. The new sales model is about asking, "What can I do to support you and solve your problems?"

- Think of a person or organization you might collaborate with to solve the problems of your Favorite Customers. List the pros and cons of doing that. If the pros are in favor, you might consider reaching out to that person or organization regarding a potential alliance. The result should be a win-win for both of you.

MOVING FORWARD FROM YOUR SOUL

- Try to think the way your Favorite Customers think. If your job is to help them succeed, consider anticipating and solving their problems before they ever come up. For example, if your customer lives in a hurricane zone, consider offering them backup software programs or twice the usual order several months before the start of the hurricane season. They'll thank you for your prescience.

Step Five: Create a Marketing Image for Your Customers

I have witnessed the softening of the hardest of hearts by a simple smile.
—GOLDIE HAWN

The outer leaves of the artichoke are spiky and sharp.

Inside the artichoke, however, is a delicate and delicious heart.

Once the outer leaves and choke are removed, the inner heart can be savored.

Like the artichoke, many people have an exterior that seems formidable or unapproachable.

Would you like your customers to see the heart-based place inside of you?

THE IMPORTANCE OF IMAGE

We now know more about ourselves and our offerings and what makes us special. We know what we do. We know who we want to attract. We know exactly what problems we can solve for our prospective customers. We even know how to *tell* people what we do. The next step in The Preparation Stage is to create an image for our *Favorite Customers* to see and a voice for them to hear.

Today's customers are smart and well educated. They dislike feeling manipulated by advertising, marketing, and sales techniques. In fact, when they're ready to purchase a product or service, they deliberately seek out a person or an organization they feel an affinity with.

These customers are pelted daily with visuals and sound bites from newspapers, magazines, television, the Internet, radio, and voice messaging systems. They often make a decision about buying something or partnering with someone based on their first impression. In doing so, they are checking out how a visual or sound bite fits their perception of themselves and what they need. They are also checking out how the marketing approach makes them "feel."

Prospective customers often make a decision about whether or not to reach out to you or your organization the *very first time* they see your photo, hear your voice, or read something you've written. In fact, this may be the *only* chance you ever have to reach this customer!

If this is the case, what would you like your customers to see, to hear, and to read about you?

CHOOSE WHAT YOUR CUSTOMERS WILL SEE
Let's create a caricature of Donald J. Trump… just for fun!

In most photos, his potential customers see a comb-over hairdo, bushy eyebrows, and a stern, almost smug facial expression. They also see him in a well-cut suit and a power tie. These features are what differentiate him from everyone else! They have become his trademark. It's how he wants to be seen… on his book covers, in his advertisements, and in his boardroom.

In a nutshell, he looks stern, tough, unconventional, powerful, and successful… which is exactly the way he wants to be seen!

On the other hand, consider a caricature of Suzanne Somers. Can't you just picture her yellow-blonde hair piled on top of her head or well-coifed with long bangs coming all the way down to her kohl-lined eyes?

Do the words sexy, fit, impish, vibrant, and healthy come to mind? If they do, she'd be mighty pleased… because that's exactly what she's selling! The diet books, the exercise equipment, and the cosmetics line are simply the vehicles!

Now, consider this… if you are a young thirty-something male consumer and you're looking for a dating service that will work for you, wouldn't you be excited to see that the CEO is a young and attractive woman in her twenties? Wouldn't you think that this woman is *in the know* about matters of dating and that she will know *many other attractive people,* just like herself, who can be potential dates for you?

On the other hand, if you're a fifty-something male transitioning executive… wouldn't you be calmed by the photo of another fifty-something gentleman overseeing an outplacement firm that claims to place mature career hunters in great number?

You get the idea.

What can we learn from this? Every visual we choose will send a message to our Favorite Customer.

So as you're creating your materials, imagine your prospective customers visiting your web site, viewing your photo, or reading your brochure or business card. Imagine them trying to get a feel for you and your business.

What messages do you want your visuals to send?

Do you want your photo to show you as a professional? Or would you prefer your Favorite Customers to see you as playful and casual? Will your attire show you as polished and well-heeled, or do you prefer to be seen as natural and clean-cut? How about your pose? Will it show you as a power-figure standing beside an executive desk, or as an old softie with a puppy on your lap?

Guess what? You get to choose!

CHOOSE WHAT YOUR CUSTOMERS WILL HEAR

Think about times you've called a company and received a "canned" voice mail message:

"Thank you for calling us today. We're sorry we are not here to take your call, but your call is important to us. We are either with a customer or busy on another line. Please leave a message."

Now it's not as if there's something *wrong* with this message… it's just that you've heard it a million times and it no longer sounds genuine or personal.

What can you do with *your* voice mail message that will differentiate you from your competitors?

Each voice mail message has its very own tone. Some are professional and dignified… others are cheery and light.

Each voice mail message leaves a caller feeling one way or another. Do you want to leave your callers feeling upbeat? If so, leave an enthusiastic message inviting them to visit your web site and promising to call them right back. Allow your personality to shine right through the phone.

Now think about creating other opportunities for your Favorite Customers to hear you. Smart marketers realize that hearing an audio message on a web site leaves visitors feeling as though they have personally met the business owner of the site. It is a great way for prospective customers to get a feel for you.

They listen to your voice… your diction, your tone, your vocabulary… even to the way you put your words together. They listen for your energy level and for your enthusiasm. Often their reaction to your voice will determine whether or not they take the next step.

If you don't yet have an audio piece for your web site, consider creating one. Potential customers expect to be able to get an accurate feel for you before they ever reach out. The audio piece will help them get to know you.

DARE TO BE DIFFERENT WHEN CREATING YOUR MARKETING IMAGE

As you're creating or redesigning your marketing materials for your Favorite Customers... think about what makes you and your business unique... and then capitalize on that with creative use of fonts and colors.

If you own a business that is targeting the corporate market, you may wish to use the businesslike colors of blue and gray in your materials.

If, on the other hand, your organization creates natural cosmetics for the teen crowd... you might try using bright pink and orange on your brochure... with flashing flowers popping across the cover. This will guarantee your prospective customer's attention!

Advertising specialists have long known the power of color choices, font choices, word choices, and musical choices. Now you will, too.

CHOOSE YOUR COLORS CAREFULLY

Let's begin with the selective use of color... on your web site, on your brochure, on your business card, and on your stationery. Using the following chart, what colors represent the brand image *you* wish to create?

- Red—forceful, dramatic, proud, strong, bold, passionate
- Orange—joyful, light-hearted, vocal, gleeful, spontaneous
- Blue—decisive, inspiring, peaceful, meditative, calming, IBM
- Yellow—intellectual, engaging, fun-loving, exuberant, expressive
- Green—balanced, healing, caring, helping, growth, lushness

The use of red can connote power, boldness, and fearlessness. The use of orange and yellow can suggest happiness, playfulness, and fun. Throw in some blue to create a professional and business-like look. Add a touch of green to create a feeling of calmness.

CHOOSE YOUR FONTS CAREFULLY

Just as color makes a statement, so does the font you use when creating your marketing pieces. Book publishers and graphic designers have been using this trick for years. Now, with computers available to most of us, we get to use it, too. Here are just a few examples of fonts I like…

- Arial Narrow—This one was introduced to me by a client who is a graphic designer… looks modern and a bit edgy… try using it in a medium gray tone

- Harrington—I like this one for my distinguished and well-polished acquaintances

- Century Gothic—Perfect for the writers among us

- Verdana—Easy to read, big enough even for aging baby boomers

- Kristen ITC—Fun for the teen crowd or a summer mailing

- Lucida Calligraphy—Great for invitations and a chic, yet casual, look

Will any of these fonts speak to your potential customers?

If not, how about looking at a few dozen more? Simply open a blank Word document on your computer, look to the drop-down box at the top of the computer screen, and select from dozens of fonts. You can choose the size of the font, too. And if that's not enough, you can buy a software package that will offer you hundreds more!

How much fun is this?

NOW IT'S YOUR TURN!

I can't imagine more fun than creating or re-creating the image you want to present to your public right now!

"But my parent company requires that I use only authorized marketing materials," you say. Well, fine. You may not have the authority to change everything… but there must be some materials within your control. If so, choose those materials to redesign!

Or, "I already have my business cards and web site and brochure," you say. Okay, but often it is inexpensive to make changes to those materials when they are not exactly what you want. Go ahead and choose the ones that no longer work… and have some fun!

The only way to find out what's great and what isn't is to lay out all of your marketing materials on the floor.

These materials may include the following, and more: business card, logo, stationery, brochure, welcome packet, personal photos, newspaper ads, magazine ads, giveaways such as pens and magnets… even the printed pages of your web site.

Look at each photo, image, and color. Look at the size and shape of your materials. Now look at each font… its form as well as its size.

Next, listen to all your audio messages, including your voice message on your answering machine, cell phone, and any other audio pieces you're using.

Are these the images and sounds your Favorite Customer will respond to? If so, you're ready for the next step. If not, go ahead and have some fun!

Redesign your image… your look, your voice, and your words! And if you need some help, there are many, many professionals out there just waiting to help you!

AN INVITATION TO YOUR TARGET MARKET

Whatever you choose in the way of visual, audio, and written messages, your main goal is to have your Favorite Customers feel comfortable approaching you. You want to invite them… in the easiest possible way… to explore a possible relationship with you or with your organization.

Because once they do, the possibilities are endless!

This Week's Action Plan

*This week is about creation…
about designing an image for your Favorite Customers to see and to hear
that will invite them to approach you with ease.*

MOVING FORWARD FROM YOUR HEART
- Have you ever been told that you seem tough or unapproachable? If so, is that how you want to be seen? You *can* get in touch with that warm, tender core inside of you. Sometimes we do need to be tough… or appear strong… but not always. If you have the need to appear strong at all times… can you consider letting that go?

MOVING FORWARD FROM YOUR MIND
- Go ahead and lay out all your marketing materials and telephone scripts on the floor. Look them over carefully, with a discriminating eye. Do they represent you in the way you wish to be represented… right now today? What still works? What needs changing? Take one big step to redo the materials that are within your jurisdiction. Perhaps you will hire a photographer to do an updated photo shoot. What will you do?

MOVING FORWARD FROM YOUR BODY
- Go ahead and listen to your recorded voice messages today. How do they make you feel? Are they inviting… or boring? Do they convey energy… or lethargy? Record your messages over and over again until you have exactly the tone and speed and message you desire.

MOVING FORWARD FROM YOUR SOUL

- This week's activity is about reviewing what makes you unique… and why your customers want *you* and *just you!* And then it's about transferring that uniqueness… in a daring and bold way… onto your marketing materials… so that exactly the right people will be wildly attracted to you!

Step Six:
Reach Out to Your Favorite Customers

> *Money and time are the heaviest burdens of life...*
> —SAMUEL JOHNSON

The world is ready to see you, to hear you, and to experience you.

The creation of a written marketing plan provides you with a way to document your step-by-step action plan.

In this step, you'll be deciding how, when, and where to get your marketing message out into the world.

The fun continues!

BEFORE YOU REACH OUT... LET'S GET PLANNING!

Deborah owns a business that offers child care for toddlers. She knows that her Favorite Customers include moms, dads, and grandparents.

She has targeted a number of venues to reach these potential customers. Among them are Parent-Teacher Organizations, soccer groups, and real estate companies that offer Welcome Packages to new home buyers.

Her plan is to reach out to these groups to inform them of her services. She has created a number of marketing materials directed to these groups, including a welcome letter, a brochure, and a video. Her neighbor, Mike, a college student, is home for the summer and helping her with marketing.

THE MARKETING PLAN
Here's a sample of what her pre-summer and summer marketing plan might look like.

Action	Date	Who
New Brochure to Parent-Teacher Organization	May 1	Deborah
Video to Soccer Moms	May 1	Deborah
Welcome Letter to New Home Owners	June 15	Mike

A marketing plan sounds a lot scarier than it is. It is simply a list of action items that represents your marketing efforts during a specific period.

Let's use Deborah's first item as an example. There are many steps leading to completion of the first marketing activity.

1. Deborah may need to get permission from the Parent-Teacher Organization to use their list.
2. She may need to edit the new brochure before printing.
3. Then, she may need to contend with printers and their timelines and any other number of situations.

Her due date for this project is clearly stated, so she will most likely be starting her work on this item several months before the May 1st date. Mike's role in the marketing plan must be scheduled around his homecoming from college. He will write the Welcome Letter in early June, have it approved by Deborah, and have it in the mail by June 15th.

In my Franchise Coaching Systems business, my assistant and I might be working from a sample plan for the month of January that looks something like this:

Action	Date	Who
Update Franchise Master List	Jan. 10	Asst.
Postcard to Assistant for Franchise Mailing	Jan. 17	Flo
Postcard to Mailing List	Jan. 22	Asst.
Newsletter to Franchise List	Jan. 29	Flo

Let's look at the action steps for item #2... the postcard mailing.

1. Create and order postcard on Vistaprint.com
2. Have postcards sent to assistant
3. Have assistant create labels and purchase postage
4. Assistant affixes labels to cards and sends
5. Returned postcards sent to assistant
6. Assistant updates database

You see? Lots to do for just one item on the plan... even in the slowest of months!

The idea here is to create a flow of marketing efforts that will move you through the entire year... even when you're at your busiest. This is the best way to keep your sales pipeline full.

And when your business is slow... that's a great time to create new brochure content or new business cards. You might also write an article or two for potential publication. The goal is to take advantage of the down times and make them productive.

The marketing plan is meant to be a work in progress. As with any plan, it may need to be reworked or adjusted for any number of reasons. It is best to create your plan for the entire year and adjust it monthly or quarterly as needed.

PLANNING AHEAD

It's great to be able to plan out your marketing activities for the whole year in advance. Here are a series of categories to consider, and questions you might ask yourself in each category. This, too, can be a fluid list. You will be adding and changing categories and questions continually.

Revenue
- What is my revenue goal for this year?
- How do I expect to meet this goal?
- What percentage of my revenue do I expect to put aside for marketing?

Research
- How can I find the names and addresses of potential customers in my target markets?
- Are there mailing lists I can buy?
- Where do I get them?
- How much do they cost?

Marketing materials
- Are my marketing materials up-to-date?
- Who can help me revise them?
- What materials do I need to order for the year?
- Do I want to try something new… like a postcard?

Venues
- Are there new venues for me to consider, such as online directories or print magazines?
- Are there speaking opportunities I'd like to seek?
- Is it time for a direct mail campaign?
- Will I create this myself or have someone else do the work?

Events
- Should I create a special event or promotion this year?
- Are there conferences or networking events I should attend?
- Should I take advantage of holidays to create special offerings?
- Do I wish to do an anniversary special?

Technology
- What use will I make of technology this year?
- What would I like to learn in this area?
- Who can teach me what I need to know?
- Can I afford to hire that person?

TAKING ACTION

Once your list of questions is compiled, it's time to find the necessary resources to move you forward. You're not expected to know how to do all of this stuff yourself, but there are lots of good experts out there waiting to help.

The secret is finding the right specialists at the right price point. Ask around for referrals for each task. Look for *The Magic Click!* with your service professionals. Does it feel easy to talk to them and to get the information you need? Are they within your budget? If so, go for it!

If there's anything I'd like to leave with you, it's this:

Marketing is forever.

You will be doing marketing activities during every month of the year for the rest of your business life!

Why?...because, even when your business is thriving, customers come and customers go.

And when they go, you want to have good prospects waiting in line to take their places.

This Week's Action Plan
This week is about planning and taking actions.

MOVING FORWARD FROM YOUR HEART

- Are you the type of person who likes to plan well in advance? If so, you will love creating your marketing plan for the year! If not, this planning thing may feel heavy or non-essential to you. What can you do to make this task more enjoyable? Can you start by brainstorming with a pal who is artsy and creative… and then ask for the support of a detail-oriented friend to finish it up? Maybe you can go online and get some ideas!

MOVING FORWARD FROM YOUR MIND

- True entrepreneurs often *abhor* the idea of putting plans in writing. If you're one of these individuals, please accommodate me by considering a shift in your thinking. Here's why. Even though entrepreneurs are typically best at creating visions and strategies, *someone* has to do the detail work. In any small business, there are lots of hats to be worn. Unless you have an employee or consultant who can wear the Detail Hat… *you* will be wearing it… along with the Vision Hat and the Strategy Hat.

- If you are a true entrepreneur, please consider this: commit to creating a 3- to 6-month "mini" marketing plan. Move your thoughts out of your brain and onto a piece of paper.

- Just trust me on this!

MOVING FORWARD FROM YOUR BODY
- Nothing helps the body more than lightening its load. Do you know how often we hold all our information in our heads? No wonder we get headaches and migraines!
- Here's a tip: Take a few minutes to do a "brain dump" every single morning when you wake up. Keep a journal nearby, or use your computer, and write down every single thought that's in your head. Then, put the thoughts into categories, or computer folders, so you can revisit them when you're ready to work on a project.

- This saves your brain from being overtaxed and your budget for pain pills from being depleted.

MOVING FORWARD FROM YOUR SOUL
- Your marketing plan is the lifeblood of your business. It keeps you moving forward even when you don't know where you're going. It can save you from despair when you have no idea what lies ahead.

- Think of the marketing plan as a map for your journey. If you're traveling down a road that branches off in three directions, and you're feeling lost or confused, take out the map. It is sure to move you forward… somewhere you *want* to go!

CONNECTION STAGE

♡ Click

Step Seven: Greet Your Favorite Customers Everywhere!

New evidence shows that the heart produces a cardiac energy. This energy may be exchanged when people make contact with loving intent. The energy that is sent registers in the reciprocal person's brain. In other words, we can literally "touch" the hearts of others just by getting close.
—KYLE RODERICK (ABRIDGED)

In this step, we're going out into the world to do the dreaded deed... we're going to network! If we're smart, we'll take advantage of opportunities to be with groups of people who fit the profiles of our Favorite Customers. If educators are part of our target market, we might attend a National Education Association event. If mothers are part of our target market, we might seek out a Parent-Teacher Organization meeting. The idea here is to find a lot of potential Favorite Customers in one place.

It's all about making contact.

THE BEST PLACES TO MEET YOUR FAVORITE CUSTOMERS

So, where to begin? Well, think of this as a very important treasure hunt. Let's imagine that one of your prospective Favorite Customers has the following profile: female, age 30 to 60, professional, and entrepreneurial. Where might you find her?

She could show up at meetings of professional organizations or networking groups, but she is just as likely to be found at the gym or the neighborhood coffee bar. You might, in fact, become acquainted with her for the first time when she is featured in your local newspaper!

Let's make a list of all the places you might run into this very valuable prospective customer. Your list might look something like this:

- Networking groups
- Professional organizations
- Industry conventions
- Chamber of Commerce meetings
- Religious and spiritual organizations
- Trendy lunch haunts
- Coffee bars
- The gym
- The club
- Bookstores
- Lectures
- Industry-specific trade journals
- Newspaper articles
- Magazine articles

I'll bet you can think of many more.

Do this exercise for each of your Favorite Customer types. List all the places you might see them, hear them, or read about them. Write your findings in your Journal.

Done? Good work! This is the easy part! Because once you find them… then you have to *do* something!

THE CARE AND SHARE

Imagine introducing yourself to a potential customer or referral source for the first time. You may experience a combined sense of curiosity, excitement, and fear!

Imagine, too, that this first conversation with a brand-new potential customer or referral source is no different than a first conversation with *any* individual… although a bit more professional.

In this professional networking situation, your means of introduction is essential to the conversation's success.

Despite participation in many networking events, I have rarely heard an introduction that sounded authentic… or that encouraged me to want to know that person better.

Each of us should be able to introduce ourselves to a new person in a way that immediately tells them what we do. But isn't it even better if we can do this in a way that shows them that we care about them as a human being, too?

Welcome to the Care and Share… a professional, warm, and thoughtful approach to the introduction dilemma.

It might be helpful to set a few intentions for your Care and Share. One intention may be to create a *real connection* with the person or group you're introducing yourself to. This is best accomplished when you speak and act in a way that is easy and authentic for you, rather than scripted or rehearsed.

You may have just a minute or two to create your impression… so the words, tone of voice, eye contact, and body language you choose all count.

The "caring" part of your Care and Share can be as simple as starting with a smile. A smile is a universal symbol of friendliness and caring.

Then, simply speak as you normally do, with easy, unforced language.

A genuine and easygoing introduction will show your new acquaintances you are genuinely happy to be meeting them.

Remember, your new acquaintance is wondering: "Who are you? What do you do? What products or services do you offer? Why should I invite *you* into my life?"

The "sharing" part of your Care and Share will help your listeners get a feel for you and what you offer. It will sound authentic and unrehearsed.

And when it comes from your best place… your heart… your listener will clearly recognize it as an honest exchange.

CRAFTING THE CARE AND SHARE

Your Care and Share might consist of 3 or 4 sentences, each answering a specific question, linked together to form a single paragraph. For example:

Sentence 1 will answer the question:

- Who are you?

Sentence 2 will answer the question:

- What do you do? What do you offer?

Sentence 3 will answer the question:

- Why should I invite you into my life?

Sentence 4 is a summary statement, as in:

- Thank you for listening.

Here's what a Care and Share might sound like for me:

- Hi! I'm Flo Schell. It's nice to meet you!

- In my work with business owners, I've noticed that so many business owners really dislike the notion of selling themselves and their services.

- My job as their Sales Coach is to help those owners find their unique selling voice… a voice that allows them to be authentic and comfortable.

- Thanks for taking a moment to get acquainted.

Here's another:

- Hello! I'm Flo Schell, Founder of Franchise Coaching Systems.

- I work with franchise owners who are ready to grow their business but feel nervous about selling.

- I love to sell and I want others to become successful at selling, too. My aim is to help these owners create a sales process that is comfortable for them *and* for their customers.

- If you know of someone who might benefit from my services, will you let me know? Here's my business card. Thanks!

YOUR TURN!

Now it's your turn. To get started, try answering *all* of these questions in your *Journal* as succinctly as possible:

- Who am I?
- What exactly is it that I do or offer?
- What problems do I help people or organizations overcome?
- How do I help them overcome their problems?
- Why do I do what I do?
- Why should someone feel comfortable inviting me into their life?
- How can I display, through words and actions, my caring for my work and for the customers I serve?

Now translate your answers into a Care and Share that follows the four-sentence format above.

How about trying your first Care and Share right here?

1.

2.

3.

4.

Are you happy with it? If so, great! If not, try writing some more in your Journal. Keep writing until your Care and Share is just the way you want it. It may take several days of coming back and refining.

The Care and Share is about giving a person a *feel* for you. It's about letting them know that you're comfortable in your skin. It's about letting them know you love your work and the people you work with. And it's about giving them a reason to either buy from you or refer others to you.

It's best created with simple words that have meaning for you, rather than rhetoric or corporate-speak. It's meant to be about what you do for others… so be careful of using the word "I" too much. And it's delivered best when it's refined and practiced over and over again… and when your eye contact is direct and warm.

It's as simple as that!

REACH OUT AND TOUCH

Okay… I hear you saying, "Caring is one thing, but sharing is quite another!" The idea of actually creating a conversation with potential customers or referral sources can give some of us stomachaches! The extroverts among us are smiling away. They're saying, "Piece of cake!"

As for the rest of us… this is where we begin to break down. And, trust me here, the very best of us struggle with this!

The good news is that we don't *all* need to "reach out and touch" in the same way! Some of us are more comfortable reaching out to new networks through e-mail or personal notes.

Others feel best meeting new people in a crowd, while still others prefer to meet people one-on-one.

What I know for sure is that there are tips and strategies for effective networking that will work for *all* personality types. The secret is to know and understand *your* personality type… and then learn to use it to your advantage!

To learn more about your personality type, you might wish to take an assessment like the Myers-Briggs Type Indicator or the DISC Personal Profile System. You might also choose to purchase Dr. Carol Ritberger's book, *What Color Is your Personality?* (www.ritberger.com) One of my favorites and great fun!

But my guess is you already know if you're an introvert, an extrovert, or someone in-between. And since you do, you'll have a better chance of creating a networking and connection style that is authentic for you.

Because here is what I know for sure: the day will come when you will simply have to make a connection with someone you don't know… whether you want to or not.

Let me offer you some tips on how to make the most of *your unique* personality type.

EXTROVERTS

If you're an extrovert, you're easy! You are generally happy to reach out to people and create new conversations. You might begin by finding out where the industry groups for your Favorite Customers meet. These events are typically listed in your local newspaper. Then, get out to as many events as possible.

I have found it *really* helps to set an intention for the outing. For example, you might create a goal such as this for the event: "I plan to have a meaningful conversation with at least three new individuals, and I plan to exchange business cards and hellos with at least four others."

Or you might say, "I hope to make three meaningful new connections tonight."

As you progress through the meeting, you'll want to be sure that the individuals you target understand who you are and what you do. You should be able to deliver this information in a short and compelling way. This is when you'll use your Care and Share.

After your introduction, consider suggesting an action that will allow you to get to know each other better. Or, if it is appropriate, offer your assistance in some way.

For example, you might offer your new acquaintances a painless, no-obligation way to get to know your services better. Perhaps you can hand them your business card with an offer for a free consultation.

Then, thank them for their time. Tell them you'll be following up by phone in a week or so to keep the connection alive. And then, no matter what, reach out and touch that individual through the telephone wires *exactly* when you promised them you would!

Remember, your goal is to begin a new relationship and to move it forward… in the easiest, most comfortable way possible.

That is the power of connection!

INTROVERTS AND IN-BETWEENS
Well, that scenario sounds easy enough for our extroverted types, but right now the rest of you are saying, "Ouch!"

So, if you're an introvert or someone in-between, how can you handle a networking event? How can you at least get the ball rolling?

Well, allow me to let you in on a secret! There really is an easy and reliable technique that will guarantee you can talk to an absolute stranger immediately upon meeting her or him… with little or no angst.

THE QUESTION/QUESTION TECHNIQUE
I've heard it called the "Question/Question Technique"… Here's how it goes:

- Person #1 (that would be you) turns to Person #2 (that elusive person you want to meet)… and simply asks Person #2 a question.

   The easiest way to accomplish this is to start with the words *who, what, when, where,* or *how*.

   The question might be about why that person came to the meeting, what company they're with, where they drove in from, how many years they've been associated with the group, or what they had for dinner and whether or not they liked it. You get the idea!

   And then your job, Person #1, is to simply listen *really carefully* to their answer.

   You'll be listening for things you have in common with this person… places you've both lived in, experiences you've both had, or foods you both like.

   The idea here is simply to form a connection. That's all there is to it!

- Once Person #2 responds completely, we'll hope she or he will ask you a question back, as in, "So, have you ever been to this group before?"

If that happens, answer the question as fully as possible… opening as much room for connection as possible.

If it doesn't… don't stop there. Go ahead and ask another question… perhaps a very open-ended one this time… a question like:

- Person #1: "What do you find the most challenging about a networking event like this?"

This question is geared toward keeping the conversation flowing… and to giving you more information about this person.

Before you know it, Person #2 will almost assuredly find a question to ask you in return and you'll both be off and running.

AN EXAMPLE

Here's an example of how the Question/Question Technique might play out:

- Person #1: Hi! What did you think of dinner tonight?

- Person #2: Well, it was pretty good. I've been here before. The food is usually reliable. How about your dinner?

- Person #1: I enjoyed it too… although I pretty much enjoy anything when I don't have to cook it myself! Do you like to cook?

- Person #2: Not my thing… but luckily my wife loves to. She comes from a big Italian family and they're cooking all the time.

- Person # 1: Lucky you! My best friend is Italian… and I know what you mean! By the way, can you recommend a good Italian restaurant in town?

You can see how it works! I just know that even the introverts among us can survive this one... maybe even learn to enjoy it over time!

Keep in mind that the information regarding what you do for a living will come up sooner or later... once you and this person have become better acquainted.

You will then have an opportunity to use your Care and Share and to tell the other person what you do and why they might want to work with you or refer you to others!

This is a technique you can use time and time again... at networking meetings, in the gym, at the beauty salon, and in the coffee shop.

THE SECRET IS THIS

The secret is this... *really* listen to what the other person is saying when they answer your questions. Remember, listening = caring. And listening carefully is how you will find commonalities to explore together.

And then, once you've found a commonality, capitalize on it. Ask a question. Share a story. Smile!

When people find meaningful connections, they ease up and the conversation becomes more natural.

(And don't forget to exchange business cards and create a method of follow-up!)

Now *your* method of follow-up may be a little different from the extrovert's method. You may not choose to pick up the phone to reconnect. But you might be okay with jotting a personal note telling that person you enjoyed meeting them and would like to stay in touch.

Or, you might feel comfortable sending off an e-mail with that same information.

The method is not important… the important thing is doing *something* to keep the connection alive!

So the secret is out… the Question/Question Technique is universally easy for all personality types… and is a strategy worth using time and time again.

OTHER CONNECTION STRATEGIES FOR INTROVERTS AND IN-BETWEENS

There are other strategies, too for you less-than-outgoing types. Here are some other ideas for connection that honor the personality styles of introverts and those who are in-between:

- Listen really carefully as people speak, then respond by simply acknowledging what you've heard.

- Post a business card or two wherever you find a blank bulletin board.

- Simply smile, say "Hi," and see where that goes.

- Send an introductory letter to someone in your target market and invite a response.

- Introduce yourself to a new person or organization by leaving a pleasant voice mail message… remembering to place a smile in your voice… and a healthy dose of energy. No matter which way of connecting feels best for you, the trick here is to stop analyzing it and to just begin doing it!

This Week's Action Plan
This week is about getting out there and doing things!

MOVING FORWARD FROM YOUR HEART

- Today's the day to begin writing several versions of your Care and Share in your Journal. Take some quiet time to start writing. Write down the answer to each of the four questions above in as many ways as you can think of. Say them aloud. How do they "land" for you? Do they sound sincere? Have you made it clear that you come from a place of integrity and customer service? Have you used words and phrases that differentiate you from your competition?

- Now try weaving the sentences together. Try them out on others. Listen to their responses. Come back and regroup, if needed.

MOVING FORWARD FROM YOUR MIND

- Our minds are great at either moving us forward or keeping us stuck in our tracks. If you believe that what you think is what you get… then you know the power of positive thoughts.

- Purchase a book of daily readings dedicated to keeping you positive. Read it during your quiet time in the morning, and it will help you to move positively through your day. There are many readers to choose from, too, from inspirational writers such as Dr. Wayne Dyer and Cheryl Richardson.

MOVING FORWARD FROM YOUR BODY

- Feeling stuck about going out into the world and talking to people? First, go easy on yourself. This public speaking stuff is notoriously feared. Then look at what's really holding you back. Is it fear of sounding uninformed? Fear of not knowing what to say? Fear of being judged? All of the above? More?

- Write your fears down… all of them. Then take a close look at them. Can you reduce the risk in any of these areas? Can you practice out loud in front of a mirror? Can you tape record your introduction and listen to it until you like the way it sounds? Can you try it out on a friend? Take a deep breath… and move forward.

MOVING FORWARD FROM YOUR SOUL

- Sometimes our most inner core contains stories we've latched on to, or even made up, over the years. These may be stories about how we can't do something, or how we should refrain from bragging or speaking up. In any case, take a look at *your* inner stories… the ones you've been telling yourself for years. Isn't it time to give up some of those stories… and replace them with stories that serve you better today?

- Need help? Try reading Cheryl Richardson's book, *Stand Up for Your Life*. It's one of my favorites!

Step Eight:
Create the Magic Click!
& Move the Relationship Forward!

*Humans are social animals.
Whenever two or more are gathered, there is opportunity for celebration.*
—AUTHOR UNKNOWN

Our work is not over once we muster the courage to network!

In fact, our goal is to create an entire series of conversations with people in an effort to find exactly the right customers for our business.

We'll know the fit is right when we experience *The Magic Click!*

Then, when we do, we will transform that initial *Click!* into a full-fledged and fruitful relationship.

THE CONNECTING CONTINUES

The connections we form with our prospective customers will occur in a variety of ways. Since we're now using all our redesigned marketing materials to get ourselves out into the world, many of our initial inquiries will be coming in by telephone in response to an ad we've placed, a brochure we've sent, or a prospective customer's visit to our web site.

In a case such as this, our prospect may already have an idea of what we offer and be eager to learn more.

They are ready to decide if what we have to offer is what they want to buy.

There is something wonderful about starting a conversation with a brand-new acquaintance. The give-and-take of notions and ideas opens us immediately to a sense of "possibility." When we're having a conversation that comes from our heart and connects us with the heart of someone else, it's simply the best!

Just as we increase our chances for success at a networking event by setting an intention and using a carefully orchestrated Care and Share, we can do the same for our initial phone conversation.

If we approach a conversation with a prospective customer with an intention to create a real connection… and if we speak from a place of curiosity and lightness… we are likely to create exactly the type of conversation we're hoping for.

Remember, our first conversation with a prospective customer is about mutual discovery. Our potential customer is asking, "Is this connection a good fit?"… and we are asking ourselves the same question.

Now let's orchestrate a very special structure for this get-acquainted process.

THE INITIAL CONVERSATION

Your *big* sales and marketing goal is to create as many inquiries as possible for your business, and to convert those inquiries into new customers.

The initial conversation following an inquiry plays a big role in your success.

There is more than one objective for this conversation. You will want to do the following:

- Listen more than you speak.

- Use a three-question approach geared toward understanding your prospect's needs and exciting and informing them succinctly about your business offerings.

- Look for opportunities to create *The Magic Click!*

- Handle your initial conversation fearlessly by using a carefully crafted "Cheat Sheet."

- Handle the money question with ease.

- Move the relationship forward in a comfortable way and take your prospect to the next step.

CREATE THE MAGIC CLICK!

As your initial conversation unfolds, you are given an opportunity to uncover things that you have in common with your prospective customer.

- Did you grow up in the same area?

- Do you root for the same team?

- Are you each an only child?

- Do you share a common nationality?

- Do you each know where to get the best pizza in Boston?

The idea here is to find a connection or commonality that can transition you and your prospective customer from absolute strangers to potential partners.

And as you're participating in "get acquainted" talk, you'll open yourself to the thrill of mutual discovery.

Here's how this works:

> When I was Vice President of Sylvan Learning Systems, my sales team would send any individuals who phoned in from the New York/New Jersey area my way. My staff could hear that northeastern twang in their voice. They knew that if anybody could *Click!* with this person, it would be me.
>
> Why? Simply because I grew up in New Jersey!
>
> So I'd get on the phone and the connection would begin. Before we knew it, the prospect and I were talking about food. Nothing is more fun than talking about the best places to get bagels and pizza!
>
> And as I invited the prospect to come to Baltimore to meet with me, I'd ask them to bring along some hot bagels.
>
> And they would!

When you hit on a commonality that works, you will know it. The conversation will flow more quickly, your voices will go up a pitch, your hands may begin to move, and your enthusiasm for the conversation will increase.

This feeling of connection… this intangible coupling… is known as *The Magic Click!*… that magic moment that brings two people closer together and leaves them yearning for more.

The magic lies in converting that sweet spark of a moment into a full-fledged mutual interest in one another. The goal is for both of you to leave this conversation feeling excited, curious, and eager for the next round.

Here are six steps that will help you to maximize *The Magic Click!*

1. LISTEN CAREFULLY... FROM YOUR PROSPECT'S EARS

Most of us have a style of conversation that is a direct result of our upbringing. Yes, we've refined it over the years, but it isn't easy to let go of old habits.

Consequently, we may interrupt one another, as if that is okay.
We may tell our relatives *what they need to do* in a given situation (as if it is our right). Or we may tell our friends *how they need to act* in order to be happier, healthier, and wiser.

Julio Olalla, founder and president of the Newfield Network, suggests there is a better way.

He tells us that when we converse with someone, we can listen to understand the situation or story *from their ears*. In other words, we actually put ourselves in *their* place and in *their* world, and try to understand the situation from *their* perspective.

He calls this highly effective technique "listening to someone from their ears."

As we listen to someone *from their ears,* we listen to the story from their point of view. We put ourselves into their world. We feel their pain, their pleasure, their anger, their joy.

Before we know it, we find ourselves understanding *exactly* what they mean.

This technique is quite contrary to our typical way of listening. Usually, when we're listening to someone else's story, we are already judging their comments as either correct or incorrect.

The truth is, we're almost never listening at all, let alone listening from the speaker's perspective. We are usually thinking about how we will rebut the story, or how we will tell a more impressive story.

Can you imagine how valuable this technique would be if you put it to use with your prospects?

Can you see how much easier it would be to create *The Magic Click!* using this type of communication?

Once the *Click!* occurs, the conversation takes a turn. It becomes easier, less contrived, and more open to an honest exchange of ideas.

The Magic Click! is nothing less than the main ingredient, the quintessential skill… and the heart of our sales process.

2. USE THE MAGIC CLICK! TO MOVE THE RELATIONSHIP FORWARD

Okay! You're on the phone, or speaking with someone in person, and you've created *The Magic Click!* Now what?

As a business owner or sales professional, your goal at this juncture is to build a new relationship and move it forward.

You've built relationships before.

You know that it takes trust, openness, honesty, and solid communication skills for a good relationship to form.

Right now, you have an opportunity with a new prospective customer to build on *The Magic Click!* and to move your new relationship to something more lasting.

After all, this person has reached out to you. Something about you or your organization has already attracted them. They may have liked your photo, or your audio message, or the tone of an article you wrote.

Now they're intent on finding out exactly what you can do to solve their problems… and how much it will cost them for that to happen.

It's your job to build upon *The Magic Click!* and establish a strong and meaningful relationship that can surmount any difficulties that present themselves.

3. USE THE THREE-QUESTION APPROACH

I always start a conversation with a new prospect with this question:

1. "So tell me, what encouraged you to call today?"

This question helps me to understand the immediate or urgent need of the customer.

It allows me to determine what my business can do to solve this customer's problem.

And it gives me an opportunity to listen for and create *The Magic Click!*

Then, I ask my second question:

2. "Are you very familiar with our business, or our product, or our service?"

Take some notes as you're listening to their response.

The answer to this is telling. The prospect may know someone who has been a customer of your business. The prospect may have heard about your service from a neighbor.

In any case, you may have an opportunity to use this commonality to create *The Magic Click!*

Then, regardless of whether the prospect is familiar with your business or not move on to question # three:

3. **"Are you okay with me taking a few moments to help you to get clear on what we offer?"**

When I ask the question in this way, I have never been turned down… ever!

And then I tell my own personal story.

I tell my prospect how I got involved in this business. I tell them the business was an absolute "fit" for me.

I allow them to hear the knowledge I've accrued over the years. I let them hear my genuine delight for the business.

I talk about the unique offerings of the business, and what makes those offerings special. I share my feelings about how well the business solves problems… and especially how it can solve *their* unique problem. I talk about how our business thrives in all economies… how necessary we are to the world.

I open the door for questions. I answer honestly. I let it all sink in. I invite them to learn more… to experience us in a way that feels easy. I assure them they are under no obligation.

And I cement *The Magic Click!* in every way I can.

4. USE A "CHEAT SHEET"

I have the perfect companion piece for helping the initial conversation along.

I call it a Cheat Sheet. This can be kept on your desk, or even in your pocket. It can be as simple as a large index card with a series of bullet items on it. Each bullet item will represent something you definitely want to do or say during your initial conversation.

In my past role, as Executive Director of Sylvan Learning Centers, my

Cheat Sheet might have looked something like this:

- Smile
- Create relationship
- Speak less… listen more
- Create *The Magic Click!*
- Build credibility
- Excite
- Inform
- Educate
- Bring to next step

The Cheat Sheet takes away any fear that you might forget something important… and will help you keep the conversation flowing easily.

It will help you to move seamlessly from one part of the inquiry to another.

Often, when we're excited about our business, we feel compelled to tell the prospect every single thing we know about it. In the case of the initial conversation, the opposite is true.

Less is better!

We want to give our prospects enough information to inform and excite them about our offering… but we also want to keep them curious.

We want to be aware of what's happening beneath the conversation. If we think we are losing our prospect's attention, then we probably are.

If we sense that our prospect is impatient for information about fees, then we're probably right.

And when we're finished listening and ready to speak, we'll speak in a way that allows our prospect to hear our excitement and enthusiasm for our business.

5. HANDLE THE MONEY QUESTION WITH EASE

It is my belief that price is always at the top of people's minds when they're reaching out for information… always!

Remember, we mentioned earlier that the word "money" is the most emotional word in the definition of "selling." Let's take that knowledge and put it to good use.

In my early years at Sylvan, I stayed away from a discussion of fees until a parent brought it up. My theory was that if money was not brought up as an objection by the customer, it was probably not a major concern.

Not so.

Prospective customers may not bring up the subject of fees right away, but it is definitely the elephant in the room!

So I changed my approach.

As I gave them information about our service, in response to question 3 above, I began to say something like this:

> "I know that you have many questions and much to learn about Sylvan. Please be assured that I will give you all of the information that you need… including our fees and our guarantee policy. Shall we take some time to get acquainted first?"

I love this approach. It acknowledges the elephant in the room… but doesn't let it interfere with our ability to create *The Magic Click!*

It gives us the opportunity to enjoy learning about one another… and to find that magical connection. It gives our prospect the opportunity to be less on guard and more their best, open self. And it gives both of us the freedom to bring up the subject of fees whenever it feels right.

What do you think?

Once we begin to strengthen our relationship with our prospective customer, we can bring up the difficult stuff more easily.

6. BRING THE RELATIONSHIP TO THE NEXT STEP

The next step in the business relationship will vary depending on your business.

In one of my early roles at Sylvan, the next step consisted of the parent coming in with their child for a diagnostic assessment session or a tour of the facility. If I successfully booked a diagnostic session or a tour, I had moved the customer forward to the next step.

Later, when I was VP of Sales at Sylvan, the next step meant that a franchise prospect would return our Confidential Profile Form.

In my coaching and consulting companies, the next step consists of a prospective client completing and returning a Client Information Form. When I receive that, my customer is at the next step in the process.

Your job is to bring your new relationship with your prospect to the next step in *your* sales process.

OH... THOSE NON-COMMUNICATIVE DAYS!

While you'd like to be at your best for every inquiry that comes in, I can assure you there will be some days when you won't want to have an initial conversation with anyone! You'll wake up on the wrong side of the bed or with lower-than-usual energy.

There are ways you can create support on those days. In other words, there are techniques you can use to support your low energy, rather than battle it.

Here are some suggestions:

- If you're not in a talking mood, consider writing to your prospect in an effort to move the relationship forward. For example, you might send a short but spirited e-mail to someone who called and left a message on your machine. This allows that person to feel "followed up with," and it allows you to honor your mood.

Just remember to use your Cheat Sheet, so you remember to smile while you're writing or speaking.

Trust me, it comes through!

- If the phone rings, you can choose to let the call go to the answering machine. You can return the call later, when your energy is better.

- Or, you can actually do things to bring your energy up. You might take a quick walk in the sunshine, eat a hearty snack, or put on some dance music and go for it… all options for increasing your good energy.

SEND IN THE CLOWNS

I'd like to share one special supportive energy technique that I've been using for years. It's called "Send in the Clowns." Here's how it works:

- You identify someone in your life that is famous for making you happy. You know that when you talk to this person, you're apt to laugh out loud and feel better instantly. This person becomes your Send in the Clowns person.

- When your disposition is low and you need to make an important call or attend a meeting, first call your Send in the Clowns person.

- Sometimes you'll get their voice mail message, and that alone will make you feel better. But when you get the real live person anything can happen!

- You might just catch up. You might share a story or two. When you choose the right person I can almost guarantee you'll have a laugh or two. Miraculously, your mood begins to change. You feel lighter, more grounded, more yourself.

- When your visit is complete, you will find yourself ready to take on that call or meeting.

- My Send in the Clowns person is my cousin Rosemary. No matter how bad a situation may feel Ro is able to get me laughing about it. Sometimes we laugh until we cry… but I always feel better when I'm through. When I get off the phone, my energy is higher, my mood is better, and I'm ready to tackle the telephone.

- You can use this technique whenever you have a difficult call to make, or a difficult meeting to attend.

- And you can use it when your mood is not "telephone-appropriate." It really works!

And then there are simply days when you should not be on the phone at all. As long as those days are few and far between, I suggest you just honor them. Take a day off. Re-energize yourself. Take a nap… whatever it takes to make it through the day.

This Week's Action Plan
This week is about creating meaningful conversations, and especially The Magic Click!

MOVING FORWARD FROM YOUR HEART

- Early in my sales career, I remember asking myself why some potential sales had gone the distance and others had not. The answer always came down to *The Magic Click!*

- If the *Click!* was present, the prospect and I would typically overcome the inevitable challenges that lay ahead. We figured out how to compromise and problem-solve and come to agreement. When the *Click!* wasn't present, those same roadblocks would get in the way and prevent the relationship from moving forward.

- In your Journal, make a list of all the commonalities you might share with *any* individual. For example, you and another person might enjoy the same sports, books, vacation spots, movies, foods, etc.

- Now imagine if you could create *The Magic Click!* with every prospect! What would happen to your sales then?

MOVING FORWARD FROM YOUR MIND

- Select a person who fits your Favorite Customer profile. Create a conversation. Call them, write them, or meet them in person. Let the conversation flow. Listen more than you speak. Listen "from their ears." Then just let the conversation flow.

- While you're conversing, listen for commonalities.

- When you find these commonalities, use them to create *The Magic Click!*

- Notice how the conversation flows from there. Jot down a few notes in your Journal answering these questions: What did you notice? What did you learn?

- Celebrate your accomplishment with something that makes you happy!

MOVING FORWARD FROM YOUR BODY

- Check in with your body each day this week. Keep track of your energy and confidence levels. Are they high or low? On days when either your energy or confidence feels low, choose one strategy that will help you create a supportive environment.

  Your goal is to increase your energy level or confidence level. You might choose to call your *Send in the Clowns* person… or you might get up and take a brisk walk. Perhaps you can go outside for a moment and get some sun! Keep trying different techniques to see what will work for you.

- Still feeling stuck? Log on and find a cheerful web site or a positive thought of the day. In fact, log onto www.FloSchell.com. If you go to the page titled, "About Flo Schell," you will see my laughing face cheering you on! Cheers to technology!

MOVING FORWARD FROM YOUR SOUL

- I have found that when I experience *The Magic Click!* with an individual, the relationship is likely to grow and continue for a long, long time. I can still remember *Clicks!* that occurred with certain interviewees that were seeking sales positions in my company.

  Those *Clicks!* were often the main reason those individuals were hired! And most of those individuals are people I continue to correspond with today... even though we have moved in many new directions.

- Trust me on this one... it's really important to pay attention to the *Clicks!*

Step Nine: Navigate the Land Mines & Come to Commitment

I open my mind and heart to be aware...
I must believe that whatever it is, I can handle it.
—Iyanla Vanzant

You just had a great initial conversation with a prospective customer. You created and felt *The Magic Click!*

Now you're ready to explore one another more thoroughly.
At this important juncture, your prospective customer is checking you out and assessing your business offering.

Depending on the cost of your product or service, this can be a short process or a long one.

So much can happen during exploration.

Your customers can get cold feet.

They can convince themselves they don't have enough money.

They can lose their financing.

It's as if predators are waiting at every corner to sabotage your sale.

Welcome to the world of the "land mines."

What can we do to help our prospects… and ourselves… through this volatile period in the sales process… so that we can indeed come to commitment?

A WORLD FILLED WITH LAND MINES

Picture this. The world is a big place and your prospective customers are out there roaming around in it. They are checking out your offerings. They are talking with your competitors. They are deciding whether or not they want to do business with you.

As they navigate through this bumpy world, there are *land mines*… big ferocious things that can jeopardize your sale… just waiting to go off!

The truth is that land mines are everywhere, no matter what your business. They can show up in the form of people, news events, changing dynamics, competing organizations, or simply cold feet.

Here are some forms the land mines might take:

- Your prospect loses their job. Fear sets in and the money runs dry!

- A "Shame on You" TV report exposes malfeasance in *your* parent company!

- A comparable product or service is condemned by the Food and Drug Administration or the Federal Trade Commission!

Land mines come in many shapes and sizes and can appear anywhere.

> I remember one from my corporate days. I had been working hard to bring a prospective buyer into my franchise system. In fact, I was feeling really solid about this sale.
>
> As my prospect was investigating the system and talking to other franchise owners, he decided to approach the franchisee in the neighboring county.

That franchise owner had always known the value of the neighboring territory and was hoping it would never be sold. After all, he had access to those potential clients… even though they weren't in his actual territory.

So when my prospect came around, the neighboring franchisee went into panic mode. He didn't want that territory to be sold! In fact, he told the prospect that the territory had been promised to him!

Yikes! My prospect called me up in a close to hysterical state. After all, he had just about come to his decision to move forward.

I attempted to calm him and immediately checked the neighboring franchisee's license agreement. There was no suggestion of a right of first refusal in his document. Thank goodness!

So while the franchisee's contention would not *legally* hold my prospect back from buying the territory, it did provide a new *objection* for my prospect to consider.

He imagined the worst… potential controversy… lack of support from his new neighbor… a turf war!

Fear and anxiety over this new development got the better of him. Despite my best efforts, he backed away.

The bad news is I lost this sale. The good news is I learned from it and put systems in place that greatly reduced the possibility of this happening again.

The even better news is that I now know how to help *you* guide your prospects through this navigation period so they will *step over* as many land mines as possible… not *on* them!

HOW TO NAVIGATE THE LAND MINES
So, how exactly do you do this?

First, you'll figure out which land mines are most likely to appear and circumvent them before they do.

Here's an example:

> Your prospect tells you they're really strapping themselves financially to buy your product or service. You can bet that a well-meaning friend may try to talk them out of this buying decision! You can also bet that any news of a downturn in the economy will have them running for cover.
>
> In anticipation of such events, you can take several steps to meet these objections head-on… before they ever occur. For lower-priced sales you can:
>
> - Bring up the idea of cost-effective payment plans right at the start.
> - Offer a pay-in-advance three-month pricing model at a discounted fee.
>
> And for higher-priced sales you can:
>
> - Open a discussion about a back-up plan for funding.
> - Suggest the possibility of a family loan.
> - Introduce your prospect to a reputable loan source.

Here's another example:

> Your prospect casually mentions their practice of calling the Better Business Bureau when selecting companies to do business with.
>
> You know a complaint has been lodged against your organiza-

tion. You also know this complaint may cause your prospect to flee.

You can:

- Bring this up well in advance and explain it thoroughly.
- Have ready a list of customers who have offered to serve as references for you.
- Suggest that your prospect call randomly selected individuals on this list with specific questions.

Here's a third example:

Your prospect informs you of their intention to check out your competition. You know your competition tends to be less than honest about the ways in which you differ. In fact, they have been known to tell blatant lies.

You can:

- Prepare your prospect for what they might hear.
- Help your prospect to objectively compare the organizations by giving them questions to ask in advance.
- Offer to sit down with them afterward to make sense of it all.

Now it's up to you to anticipate, navigate, and counteract as many land mines as you can... one by one.

YOU CAN DO THIS!

I know you are capable of helping your prospective customers step over most of the land mines, whatever they are.

You can do this because you have taken the time to build a strong and open relationship with your prospect. You can do this because you have solved problems successfully with your prospect already. And you can do this because you will anticipate as many of those land mines as possible… and handle them before they ever come up.

And in so doing you'll keep the enemies at bay… and your prospects alive.

If the land mine is so-o-o big that it is out of your control, you will gently let your prospect do whatever she or he will do.

Because we can't control everything!

SIDE BY SIDE

One way to manage this navigation period is to stay close to your prospect's side.

Now, I'm not suggesting that you *literally* hang out with them daily… but I am suggesting that you keep in close touch with them and act as a guide as they move through their process of exploration.

Here are some scenarios that may cause you to draw closer to your prospect:

- Your prospect is excited about your offering and is ready to talk to others who have used your products or services.
- Your prospect is ready to move forward but is waiting for his or her spouse to agree.
- Your prospect has been talking to you weekly and suddenly stops taking your calls.
- Your prospect has spent a good amount of time learning about your offering and suddenly goes away.

Well, thanks to technology, you can certainly check in with your prospect consistently by e-mail. My advice is to keep your e-mail interchanges short, casual, and curious. In other words, gently probe for ways you can help your prospect move forward and come to a decision.
Here's an example of an interchange I might create for a prospect who is not responding to my e-mails:

> "Hi. I'm missing our discussions. Getting started is often the toughest part. Is there anything I can do to help?"

If that doesn't get a response, and I really think this person could be one of my Favorite Customers, I might create a second e-mail such as this:

> "Checking in and looking forward to working with you. Is there something on your mind? If you could tell me anything right now, what would it be?"

If e-mail is not an option, you can take this same approach by telephone or snail mail. Telephone can be tough… because everybody is screening calls these days. It is very easy for prospects to avoid you if they wish.

However, a personal note is still a wonderfully intimate way to stay in touch.

MY PERSONAL ADVICE

Often a business owner or sales professional will ask me, "If my prospect seems to be avoiding me, when should I stop calling?"

My personal advice regarding prospects who are hanging out interminably in the world of the *land mines* is this:

- Stay in touch with a prospect as closely as you can without creating pressure until you hear them say, "No thank you."
- Until they say those words, give them the benefit of the doubt.
- There are so many ways that life can get in the way.
- When a prospect says, "No thank you," remove them immediately and cheerfully from your follow-up list.
- Then ask them if you can stay in touch from time to time.

SPECIAL NAVIGATION SKILLS

This journey through the land mines requires a number of special skills on your part. These include the ability to:

- Foresee potential problems
- Muster the fortitude to confront these problems with your prospect early on
- Problem-solve effectively with your prospect
- Interact honestly and openly with your prospect
- Confront and overcome fear (yours and the prospect's)
- Be persuasive in a non-threatening way
- Pay attention to your intuition, or gut, and act on that
- … and a whole lot of follow-up and commitment

Of these, I think "fear" is the biggest of them all.

CONQUERING FEAR

Let's talk about fear, because it's the new elephant in the room.

What might *you* fear?

- Hearing your prospect say "no"
- Rejection if your prospect goes away
- Disastrous results if your prospect doesn't buy
- Making follow-up calls
- That you're pressing too hard
- That you are not good enough

What might *your prospect* fear?

- Making a costly mistake
- Being sold a "bill of goods"
- The commitment of working together
- Not knowing all there is to know

While these can feel like *really big* fears… they are not impossible to overcome.

Here's what I've learned about handling these types of fears over the years.

- If you have done everything possible to build a strong relationship with your prospect and have offered the best value for their money, your prospect is likely to buy from you.

- If you have helped them navigate the landmines, offered them solutions to their concerns, and helped them come to an honest decision, they are likely to buy from you.

- If you have done everything possible to create an open and honest partnership, they are likely to buy from you.

And if they don't, it was just not meant to be.

Most probably, it was not the right fit.

That's it and that's all.

HANDLING REJECTION

We are human beings interacting with other human beings. We use all of our skills and qualities to help our prospective customer come to the best decision. It may be that at this moment in time, the best decision for our prospect is to say, "No thank you."

If that is the case, know that you have done your job well. You have walked with them along the path, you have helped them step over as many land mines as possible, and you have done what you can do.

And because you've done it well, your prospect will hold you in high esteem, come back to you when and if they're ready, and tell others about your product or service.

We can't ask for more than that!

Often, we forget all of this and walk away feeling rejected. We take the rejection personally, as if we are not good enough.

In the best-selling book, *The Four Agreements*, Don Miguel Ruiz says this:

"During the period of our education, or domestication, we learn to take everything personally. We think we are responsible for everything."

He goes on to say, "Nothing other people do is because of you… it is because of themselves."

Does this mean that we have no impact whatsoever on another person's decisions?

I think not.

But it does mean that the final choice anyone makes about *any* thing in life is based on their own "stuff"… not ours.

When a prospect says, "No," and they assuredly will from time to time, be conscious that it is about "them"… not about "you."

Truly, you don't have that much power.

YOUR PERSONAL STYLE
The manner in which you move through this exploratory and commitment period will have a direct effect on the outcome.

If you are coming from a place of fear, your prospect will feel that.

If you are coming from a place of manipulation, your prospect will feel that.

If you are coming from a place of neediness, your prospect will feel that.

And, if you are coming from your best place… from your heart… your prospect is likely to feel that, too!

In this last case, you can feel comfortable admitting when you don't know something. You can assure your prospect that you will return with an answer as soon as you're able. And you can communicate clearly that some decisions are outside of your domain.

This stage, above all others, requires a heart-to-heart connection. When you communicate clearly and cleanly, you're able to ask difficult and probing questions, and you're able to have big conversations.

There's a lot of juice in those big conversations.

In fact, it is in these big and intimate conversations that you often move the prospect forward… or accept the conclusion that this sale is just not meant to be.

COMMITMENT IS BIG STUFF
Coming to commitment is a big thing… none of us takes commitment lightly.

If we think back to the qualities we identified early on as characteristic of a long-term relationship, we know that this stage requires:

- Trust
- Honesty
- Open communication
- The ability to solve problems together
- Compromise

Your prospects will come to a decision, sooner or later, about whether or not they are willing to commit to a relationship with your business.

If they do, the fun begins! You get to take your new relationship and move it forward into a long-term and satisfying one.

And if they don't, you can ask their permission to stay in touch. Who knows… they may return when the time is right.

ENSURING COMMITMENT

There are some things you *can* do to ensure that your prospect will make it through to a successful close. You can:

- Create a timeline for your prospect's decision-making and help them to stick to it.

- Check in daily during the last stages of the buying process to see if there is anything your prospect needs.

- Make it as easy as possible for your prospect to get the resources and answers needed.

- Listen for cues, watch for body language, and use your intuition to pick up those objections that remain unsaid.

- Create an open and frank conversation about those objections.

- Handle difficult conversations with great care… and great honesty… in an effort to bring the sale to a clean close.

- Remind your prospect that they *do* know how to make good decisions… and that they've made many good decisions before.

CLOSING THE SALE

If there's anything I've learned about "closing" over the years, it is this:

- If you've done a thorough job of building a strong relationship at the outset, you will have a better chance of surviving the bumps that are sure to occur.

In other words, bumps are normal. It is the quality of your relationship that helps you overcome them.

- Prospects are human. They want to get the best price possible for the most product or service possible.

This is just human nature.

So if price is a deal breaker, and if you can give them a better price without sacrificing your values or profit margin, consider doing it.

And if you can't or don't wish to compromise your pricing structure, just say so.

- Sometimes, in the final negotiation phase, there are things you can do to make your prospect happier.

Just as often, there are things you *cannot* do.

Letting your prospect know up front that there are some things you can do and some things you cannot do is a good way to do business.

If you have built sufficient trust, your prospect will know that when you can, you will… and when you can't… well, you just can't.

This simple knowing will often be enough to move the prospect forward… even if they don't get everything they desire.

So… what can *you* do to ensure that your prospects will come to a timely and confident close?

_____

_____

_____

This Week's Action Plan
This week is about handling big decisions and coming to commitment.

MOVING FORWARD FROM YOUR HEART
- Nothing feels scarier than rejection. It feels as if "we" are being rejected rather than the product or service that we're offering. Don Miguel Ruiz's book, *The Four Agreements* (www.miguelruiz.com) can serve as a template during this period. He tells us, in the second agreement, not to take things personally… and he explains why.

    If you haven't seen this book, please consider seeking it out. It may help to keep your ego and self-esteem intact during the sales process. Understand that people make decisions for many, many reasons. These decisions have to do with things that are going on for them.

    If we take the decision personally, we suffer. If we don't take the decision personally, we thrive.

    This is simply the truth.

MOVING FORWARD FROM YOUR MIND
- Think about one big commitment you've made in your life with a personal provider or company. How difficult was it to make? What steps did you take during the exploration period? What was the deciding factor in your moving forward?

    This simple discovery may help you realize that some commitments are meant to be… and others are not. And that either way, the decision is perfect.

MOVING FORWARD FROM YOUR BODY
- Select someone in your life to interview this week. Ask them about a product or service they recently committed to. Have them review what steps they went through in coming to their decision. Then ask them this question: "What was the biggest thing that influenced your final decision?" Write those "influencers" in your Journal. Does this shed any further light on what your prospective customers are going through?

MOVING FORWARD FROM YOUR SOUL
- Your soul is that part of you that holds the greatest wisdom. As you navigate through this period in the sales process, take a moment to check in with yourself. What fears are you holding? Name them. Write them in your Journal. What can you do to lessen their hold on you? Who can help you with this?

  If you are feeling stuck in this important period in the selling process and need a dose of confidence… please accept this invitation to reach out to me via e-mail with your questions or concerns.

  Simply visit www.FloSchell.com and use the e-mail link provided. Let me know that you are in the midst of reading this book and I will respond to you as soon as I'm able.

  And while you're there, sign on for my free e-newsletters: Just go with the Flow and/or The Future of Franchising.

  After all, we heart-based sales professionals need to stick together!

LIVING TOGETHER STAGE

Click ♡

Step Ten: Be Masterful with Your Customer Relations

*Do your work with your whole heart and you will succeed…
there is so little competition.*
—E<small>LBERT</small> H<small>UBBARD</small>

You made it!

You managed the land mines.

You brought your sale to a close.

Your prospect is now on board as one of your newest Favorite Customers!

Take a few moments to celebrate this accomplishment.

In fact, plan a major celebration. You've earned it!

Now you're ready to create a relationship with this customer that will last for a long, long time.

You know that treating your customer well at every opportunity is a smart thing to do.

You also know that happy customers are apt to tell others about you.

Let's be masterful with our customer relations for the best reason, too… because it's the right thing to do!

WELCOME TO THE FAMILY

When a new customer enters my business family, I feel privileged. I know this customer has chosen me over many other service providers. And I am going to do everything in my power to treat my customer with care, warmth, openness, and integrity.

Over the years I have adopted some guidelines. I hope you will find them helpful:

- Offer your customers a written policy guide.
- Anticipate your customers' needs.
- Follow up when you say you will.
- Be available to your customers when they need you.
- Handle difficult subjects with ease and openness.
- Observe your customers' "happiness level."
- Measure your customer satisfaction.
- Go out of your way to make the partnership pleasant.
- Give a little bit of your love today.

OFFER YOUR CUSTOMERS A WRITTEN POLICY GUIDE

At some point in your sales process, you told your customers exactly what they would be getting in return for their money. You may have created a written contract of sorts or a Letter of Agreement. If not, it is wise to do this right now… at the beginning of your business relationship.

When creating a written document, I generally recommend using the term "agreement" rather than "contract." Unless you really need a legal partnership, the word "agreement" tends to be less scary… and more customer-friendly.

Your agreement will clarify your policies and the way you work. It will clearly delineate what is expected of each party. If a party doesn't honor the guidelines, it will outline the consequences that could result. Your document should contain language for resolving disputes, and language for leaving the relationship.

In short, your agreement eliminates any doubt about what the business relationship will look like. It offers a template for resolving problems… and it offers a map for your relationship.

Once your document is in place, it is wise to go over it step by step with your customer. Be sure to address any questions or inaccuracies. If something seems muddy, clear it up. Then go ahead and sign the document. Have your customer do the same. You now have a living, breathing document that serves as a guideline for your work together.

Early in my coaching business, I noticed how difficult it was for many of my customers to tell me when they were ready to leave the coaching relationship. This sometimes created a surprise ending… or even an uncomfortable one.

Once I noticed this, I resolved to make it easier for my customers to leave. I included a paragraph in my Coaching Agreement with wording such as this:

> "Should you feel ready to complete our work together and to leave the coaching partnership please bring this to my attention. My objective is that you leave with a sense of completion. To that end, I will schedule a complimentary Exit Session to ensure that any final thoughts either of us have will be shared. Thank you!"

This simple addition to my Coaching Agreement, coupled with a clear discussion about the leave-taking process, has made my customer endings much smoother.

Once your written agreement of terms is completely executed, or signed, by both parties, you can file it away. There may come a time you will want to refer to it… so keep it in your customer's individual file. And be sure your customer has a copy, too.

ANTICIPATE YOUR CUSTOMERS' NEEDS

When I think back to the best business relationships in my life, I remember my professional partners doing things such as this:

- Sending me a reminder card before my next visit.
- Keeping track of my purchases and letting me know when I might be running out of something.
- Offering me flexible hours.
- Being well stocked with my favorite products.

I feel thankful each March when Costco, one of my Favorite Businesses, maintains their stock of fire logs! While other companies stop carrying this item much earlier in the season, my Costco knows there is a strong likelihood that New Jersey will have chilly days even in May. Every time one of those days arrives and my logs are warming me, I silently thank them.

Now that I'm a business owner myself, I try to anticipate my own customers' needs. In my franchise coaching and consulting business, I remember how stressed I felt as a franchise sales executive during the last quarter of the year. In honor of my franchise customers who deal with that, I offer special tips for closing end-of-year sales. It's my way of giving back.

Similarly, I remember how difficult it felt to regroup at the start of a new year. So in January I offer a lighthearted event meant to ease franchise executives back into the fray.

Customers really appreciate it when we anticipate what they want or need.

FOLLOW UP WHEN YOU SAY YOU WILL

Nothing gets us in more trouble than promising to do something and then not following through. Often it's not purposeful, but the reaction is the same.

Most of us have daily to-do lists that are impossible to complete. We can all use help with prioritizing better and delegating more freely.

If you know that follow-up is a challenge for you, create a system that will encourage it. If you use technology, this might be a computer alarm or a pop-up box that you program into place. If you're not a techie yet, you might use a tickler system in a box that allows you to move index cards from one day to another. If you don't complete a task on one day, you can move it forward manually to the next.

There are so many techniques available, that there really is no excuse for not following up exactly when you say you will.

The secret is to select a system that works for you and then to use it!

BE AVAILABLE TO YOUR CUSTOMERS WHEN THEY NEED YOU

No matter what your business offers, you will be thanked if you are there when your customers need you.

Sometimes, in a service business, your customers will need you outside of your normal business hours. Is there a way for your customers to contact you in case of emergency? If not, is there someone else you can refer them to?

On other occasions, your customers may need you when they're having a tough day. Is there something you can offer them for those less-than-good days?

In my service-based businesses, customers typically schedule their time with me in advance. However, a customer often will have an immediate need… even though their scheduled session is not until the next week.

In this type of situation, I offer my customers "In the Moment" connection opportunities. This means they are free to phone me for an impromptu 10-to-15-minute conversation. This doesn't happen often, but when it does, my customers are relieved and grateful!

- In your business, is it possible for *you* or your staff to be readily available to your customers when they need you?
- If so, what systems can you put in place to ensure that your customers can find you when they do need you?

HANDLE DIFFICULT SUBJECTS WITH EASE AND OPENNESS

It is almost impossible to expect our relationships with our customers will be problem-free. After all, we are humans interacting with other humans… with everything this implies.

So let's enter our relationships with our customers knowing that difficult issues are likely to come up.

Since money and fees are emotionally charged ingredients of a business relationship, we can expect that difficulties might arise in these areas most of all.

> Here's a touchy situation that I dealt with recently. I sent a notice to my current customers advising them that a revised services fee schedule was in effect for new customers.
>
> I thought carefully about whether or not I would apply this new fee schedule to existing customers.
>
> My final decision was to advise my existing customers of the change and to grandfather their fees for a full six months.
>
> This felt fair to me… but I felt a pang in my chest as I sent the notices out!
>
> Several days later, my heart was telling me that my decision didn't feel so good.
>
> I thought about how I would feel in my customers' place. I decided

to have a discussion with each customer affected by this change.

One of my customers said the fee change was absolutely understandable. She was not at all concerned.

Another said she was taken aback. Her instinct was to stay on as a customer until the new fee went into effect and then leave the relationship.

I listened carefully *from their ears*. I tapped into my business mind. I tapped into my heart space.

In the end, I chose to have a good clean discussion with each existing customer. I told them I wanted them to feel comfortable staying with the relationship until they were absolutely ready to leave. I told them I did not want a changed fee structure to get in the way of their doing that.

My decision to maintain their fee schedule at the original rate brought sincere thanks. While you may choose to handle such a situation differently, I left the conversations feeling I had done the right thing.

These types of touchy subjects will continue to be part of our business relationships. However you choose to handle a situation such as this… the object is to handle it… not ignore it.

You can measure your satisfaction with your business decisions daily by asking questions such as:

- What did I learn from the way I handled this touchy situation?
- Am I happy with the outcome?
- Could I have handled this differently?
- If so, what guidelines can I put in place to avoid this happening in the future?

You can solve customer difficulties in a heart-based way by getting your customers' input and scheduling a problem-solving session where options can be explored. Then you can come to a satisfying solution together.

That's a technique that creates a win-win… and that's what heart-based businesses are all about!

OBSERVE YOUR CUSTOMER'S HAPPINESS LEVEL

It is very wise to watch for signals that might suggest your customer is feeling fidgety or ill at ease.

You can accomplish this by carefully observing your interactions with your customer and noticing if anything seems out of sorts. If you work by phone or Internet, you can listen for silences or hesitations and watch for delayed responses… or lack of response.

If you notice any unease or hesitation, don't be afraid to check in with your customer on what you're noticing. Since it's impossible to know if what you're noticing is symptomatic of a hidden problem or not, the best way to find out… is to ask!

Often a customer will be very good at hiding their concerns, disappointments, or annoyances. Many of us have been trained to be polite and to hold our tongues. If you have a feeling that something is amiss, you can take the following steps:

- Come from a place of curiosity.
- Go out on a limb and ask about it.
- Ask your question gently.
- Listen carefully to the answer from your customer's ears.
- Do what you can to make the situation better… immediately.

Your intuition is the driver here. It tells you when something may be up. The goal is to pay attention to your intuition… and to gently act on it. Customers appreciate honest inquiry.

The truth is… you will appreciate it, too.

MEASURE YOUR CUSTOMER'S SATISFACTION

Many of today's technology-savvy companies are measuring customer satisfaction by using Customer Relationship Management (or CRM) systems. The idea, in mid-size to large companies, is to ensure that everyone in the organization is concentrating on satisfying their customers.

These software systems can immediately handle customer inquiries and ensure quick follow-up.

However, not all businesses are financially able or ready to invest in such a system. There are other user-friendly approaches, such as Exit Interviews, that can ensure you know whether or not your customers have left happily.

An Exit Interview can be conducted in person or via a written form that allows customers to share their level of satisfaction with you anonymously.

Whatever your size, it is important to create an evaluation technique that allows you to know whether or not your customers left the relationship satisfied with their experience.

The truth is this: You want your customers to be *more* than satisfied when they leave you. You want them to be absolutely *delighted* with your product or service. You want them to prefer doing business with you… and only you.

And you want them to tell everyone they know about you, too.

So what can *you* do to ensure this will happen in *your* business?

GO OUT OF YOUR WAY TO MAKE THE PARTNERSHIP PLEASANT

Let's face it… your customers have lots of choices when they're selecting business partners. If they choose you, doesn't it make sense for you to go out of your way to make the relationship pleasant?

This may seem obvious, but I have experienced many less-than-pleasant buying experiences that prove not all business owners get this… and I'll bet you have, too!

> Recently I visited a delicatessen in my neighborhood. The counterpersons were behind a counter filled with delicious luncheon items.
>
> There was a list of daily specials posted. I was immediately drawn to the hot chicken soup.
>
> When it came my turn, I requested the soup.
>
> The counterperson gave me a frustrated look, pointed to a refrigerated case in another part of the store and growled, "The soup is over there."
>
> Humph! I wasn't feeling customer love!
>
> Wouldn't it be more pleasant for both of us if the soup was behind the counter with the rest of the food…so that the nasty look and comment could be avoided?

Perhaps this less-than-satisfying service experience is an example of poor training from the top. Maybe it's just indicative of this counterperson's personality… or mood at that moment. In any case, the end result is the same. With two soup-selling delicatessens right next door to one another, I will not be choosing the unpleasant sales experience again!

So, what does it take to offer your customers a heart-based and pleasant experience *each* time they see you or meet with you or your staff?

The answer is surprisingly simple. It may be as easy as giving your customer a big smile each time they come in… or a hearty hello on the telephone. Or, it may be that you offer a jar of candy or a free cup of hot chocolate.

Do you remember, at the very beginning of our journey together, how I reacted to the beautiful loaf of Asiago and potato bread I received from Joe Leone's?

There are so many ways to make your customers feel special and appreciated… even if your relationships are conducted primarily online or by telephone!

In my franchise consulting business, I like to surprise my customers occasionally with a free Advanced Open House telephone session featuring a franchising expert. They often are grateful for the experience.

Sometimes I'll send a card or a news article through the U.S. mail with a special meaning for my customer. Getting a real piece of mail these days is cause for celebration… and personalizes my relationship with that customer.

The best surprises of all can be inexpensive and require little time.

Here are some questions you can ask yourself that will help your business stand out from all the rest:

- What can I do at *every opportunity* to let my customers know I care about them?

- What can I do *every day* that is free or inexpensive and that will give my customers a sense of pleasure?

- What can I do *occasionally* that will let my customers know I am going out of my way for them?

- What types of pleasantries can I institute that feel natural and comfortable for my business?

- What training do I need to provide to ensure that my staff delivers the same excellent customer service I do?

GIVE A LITTLE BIT OF YOUR LOVE TODAY

With so much business being conducted by phone and Internet, it may seem challenging to make your customer relationships as personal as you'd like.

Despite this, it is not uncommon, particularly in service-oriented businesses, for business owners and sales professionals to create close and meaningful relationships with their customers.

After all… most of us have been known to "love" our vet, our beautician, or our handyman. Why not learn to "love" your customer as well?

Take pleasure in enjoying the real connection that occurs between two individuals who have experienced *The Magic Click!*

Because… when you're partnering with your Favorite Customers, you shouldn't be surprised when the relationship with them becomes special.

This is one of those intangible "wins" that occurs when you select exactly the right customers for your business.

(If you belong to a professional association, you should be able to find clear guidelines about how to ethically handle customer relationships. If you do not, create smart guidelines for yourself.)

This Week's Action Plan

This week is about being masterful with your word, with your follow-up, and with the way you manage the relationships of your life.

MOVING FORWARD FROM YOUR HEART

- Choose any important relationship in your life. Watch it carefully this week. How are you "being" in the relationship? Are you masterful with your actions? Are you masterful with your words? Are you going out of your way to make the relationship pleasant?

    Chronicle the health of your relationship in your Journal this week.

    At the end of the week, consider how satisfied you are with your level of mastery in this relationship.

    Give your satisfaction a number on a scale of one to ten, with ten being the highest and one being the lowest.

    What one thing can you do next week to bring your number up a notch?

MOVING FORWARD FROM YOUR MIND

- Some companies use their own satisfied customers to spread the good word to potential new customers.

    These satisfied customers might take calls or accept visits from prospective customers. They might even become spokespersons for the company.

    The best part is that potential customers get the information they need in a credible manner, directly from the customers of your business.

Do you have satisfied customers who might be willing to help you by offering a testimonial or referral? If so, what type of referral system can you create that will allow both you and your satisfied customers to "win"?

MOVING FORWARD FROM YOUR BODY

- Take some time this week to identify two to three of your Favorite Customers. Ask them how they would describe your commitment to customer service.

  If favorable, ask them if you might use their words as a Testimonial Statement. Afterward, send them a heartfelt thank you.

  If not favorable, thank your customer for their openness… and do what you can to make it right. Think carefully about *immediate* steps you can take to improve your customer service with that person.

MOVING FORWARD FROM YOUR SOUL

- How cool is it to love the people you are doing business with? Does this idea scare you… or make you smile? What can you do to open yourself to being okay with loving your customers?

  Can you reframe what the word *love* might mean to you in an instance such as this? Can you identify with other things or people you "love"… like crusty pizza, your dog, your favorite sports team?

  Create a definition that will allow you to be open and free with your affection and still maintain the highest levels of professionalism.

  We're talking common sense here… and lovingkindness.

  And integrity of the highest order.

Epilogue: When it's Time to Part... Create a Soft Landing and Stay in Touch for a Long, Long Time

> *Parting is such sweet sorrow.*
> —**William Shakespeare**

Our goal is to live with our customers for a long, long time.

And when we part… we wish for the landing to be soft and just.

FLUFF UP THE PILLOW IN ADVANCE

Eventually, in even the best of customer relationships, it will be time for our customers to part. The more we can do to soften the landing, the better!

You'll remember that in my own coaching and consulting businesses, I took several steps at the outset of the relationship to assure a soft landing.

- I added parting language to my Coaching Agreement.

- I discussed the parting process with my customers when they first entered the partnership.

After my first year in business, I added something more to my Coaching Agreement. It said this:

"If at any time our partnership is not working optimally for you, please communicate that to me. Often, we can make the necessary adjustments to have the alliance become the best it can be."

Now that gets us off to a good start! Once my customer is on board, I check in often, sometimes every week, to see if the coaching partnership is what they had hoped for.

I might ask them what value the session had for them that day. I might ask if the partnership is still meeting their needs.

My customers' answers are open and revealing. Most of the time, they will express satisfaction with the way things are going. They often mention enjoying a surprising "Aha!" And sometimes they offer thanks for getting a new perspective on a challenge they're facing.

But sometimes they'll tell me less-than-satisfying things, too.

They may say they're just not ready for the accountability that is typical of a coaching relationship. On other occasions, they may tell me they are just not able to give the coaching partnership the time it deserves.

Whatever their response, the opportunity is opened for rich conversation.

And should they feel ready to leave the partnership, I will do all that I can to allow that to happen… easily and joyfully.

READING BETWEEN THE LINES

Sometimes it's not so clear that a customer is ready to leave. So I watch for subtle hints. Perhaps my customer is suddenly canceling sessions… or coming to them late. Or maybe my customer is just not following up on the actions we co-created, and their heart does not seem to be in our work.

In your business, you may find that your customer is not answering your calls… or is hesitant about meeting with you.

When you notice these types of hidden messages, the best thing you can do is to "check in." Gentle questions work best, such as:

- Is there something else going on here?
- Is it time for us to assess our work together?
- What feels like the *absolutely right action* for you to take at this time?

My goal, for both my customer and myself, is to leave the partnership with a clear understanding of what was accomplished… and with an open invitation for the customer to return whenever that feels right.

Of course, my *big* goal is for my customer to leave the partnership feeling that their money has been well spent, and that they received even more than they'd hoped for.

What can *you* do to help *your* customers leave happily?

STAY IN TOUCH FOR A LONG, LONG TIME

Once, when I was training a sales professional I was asked, "When should I stop making follow-up calls?"

The answer I gave was, "Not until you hear the word NO."

At the time, the question was posed in the context of following up on old inquiries… in other words, leads that had gotten cold. I explained it further in this way:

"The people on our planet are busy, busy individuals. There are so many reasons a potential customer might not call us back, or might have to put us aside for awhile. Give your prospect the benefit of the doubt."

I further suggested that the sales professional check in periodically, in a cheerful and upbeat way, to see if the prospect needed any help.

I have many examples of how I learned about the importance of keeping in touch. Once, after weeks of the initial inquiry effort, I finally reached a prospect. She told me she had not yet had a chance to look over my material. I kept her on my Callback List. Another time, after continual attempts at reaching a prospect, I learned that he had not yet had an opportunity to talk with his spouse. Again, I kept him on my Callback List.

And once, in my career at Sylvan, I stayed in touch with a franchise prospect for two full years! I knew this prospect was a great fit for our business. He waited until the timing was right for him.

The truth is… the only time I take a prospect off my Callback List is when they tell me "no." This may be in the form of, "I'm no longer interested" or "Please stop calling." In any case, when I receive a definite "no," I honor it.

I feel the same way about staying in touch with former customers. Once a customer leaves, I reach out from time to time… when it feels right.

If I know their birthday, I send them a birthday card or give them a surprise call. If I see an article I think they'll find interesting, I mail it to them. If I come across a card particularly pertinent to them, I put it in the U.S. mail.

When my business is celebrating an anniversary, I may send them a Gift Certificate for a free session, or an invitation to a free "Tele-gathering."

And when I'm thinking about a former customer, I let them know… and I invite them to do the same!

THANK YOU

Well, my ardent readers, we are at the end of this leg of our journey. We have completed all ten steps in the selling process. I thank you for taking the journey with me. I hope you are feeling more than satisfied with the information you've received and the manner in which it was delivered.

I hope you will go back to some of the exercises if you skipped a few steps along the way… If you have done them all, go back and review them from time to time… you've come a long way since Step 1!

I hope you will make the material your own.

And I hope you feel better qualified than ever to sell your products and services in a way that is comfortable and authentic for you and for your customers.

It has been a joy for me to share this journey with you!

Want to connect personally? Please contact me through www.FloSchell.com.

Good-bye for now. I'll be doing my best to stay in touch… and I hope you will, too!

Happy Selling!

Parting Words, Invitations, and Respected Resources

Dear Readers,

Congratulations! You've completed all 10 steps and are well on your way to being highly successful at sales… whether you are a small-business owner or a sales professional already.

Nothing would make me happier than to continue to support you as you open your minds and hearts to this new way of being in your work and in your lives.

In the world of coaching, we know that our lives and our work are artfully mixed together. It is hard to affect one area without affecting the other. So it is safe to say that your sales relationships will prosper from using this model… and your personal relationships will, too.

I'd love to invite you to take the next step toward taking this model further.

As a special gift, I'd like to offer you the price of this book ($24.95) as a credit toward whatever step you might take. Those steps are listed on the following pages under the title, "Are you ready for some action?" This offer applies to all programs or products delivered or owned solely by the author.

You may use your credit within 60 days of purchasing of this book. It is my way of saying "thank-you" for reading, and for bringing this sales model into the world.

Now, turn the page and open the door to the wealth of opportunities that await you.

My best to you,

Flo Schell, EdM

Are you Ready for some Action?

Are you Ready for some Action?

You may be yearning for individual sales coaching at this point. If that's the case, visit the author's website to take advantage of this special offering for book readers only:

You are invited to schedule a complimentary 30-minute coaching call with the author on a topic of your choice. Please complete the short information form at:

www.FloSchell.com/ complimentarycoaching.html

Then, click "send" and look forward to hearing from the author personally.

During your initial session and with your permission, you will be given full information on how to hire the author as your coach. If individual coaching is something you pursue, you will be credited for the price of this book ($24.95) on your first month's coaching invoice.

You may be ready to participate in our 8-week Sales Coaching Program… available to you by phone in the privacy of your home or office. The Program will support you as you work on mastering the specific steps in the sales model. Get more information at:

www.FloSchell.com/ salescoachingprogram.html

To sign on for the Program, simply complete the short form and we will do the rest! Don't forget to mention your book discount.

(click)

You might decide that you'd like to continue to learn more about this sales model as part of a team. If so, consider Group Sales Coaching, in which you will become part of a "sales team" consisting of 4–8 members. Your team will participate in weekly calls over a period of 3 months. You will then have the opportunity to continue, if you wish.

If this offering is of interest, visit:

www.FloSchell.com/ groupsalescoaching.html

Book readers using the above link may request their $24.95 credit toward this offering upon registration. We hope to welcome you to the team personally soon!

(click)

In any case, you will certainly want to stay in touch through the author's free online newsletters: *Just go with the Flow,* and *The Future of Franchising.* To register, visit:

www.FloSchell.com
or
www.FranchiseCoachingSystems.com

Or you may wish to get acquainted with Flo by e-mail. If so, simply jot a note to: **mycoach@FloSchell.com.** You will receive a personal response.

Are you a Leader in the Franchise World and ready to take on more?

If you are involved as a manager or sales professional in a franchised business, or you are an owner of a franchised business, we'd like to be sure you have all possible tools and resources at your fingertips.

There are some invitations I'd like to extend to you and some resources that I think highly of. (Please note: The book discount applies only to the programs and services solely owned and delivered by the author.)

For worldwide franchise information, visit The International Franchise Association at **www.franchise.org**

If you are a manager in a franchised business, you are invited to request the services of the author for a one-day motivational seminar or sales training for your staff. These events are customized to meet your needs. Here's what some clients have to say:

> *"Flo Schell and Franchise Coaching Systems impacted our organization in a single day by reminding us that many things were already working well. This positive framework allowed us to speak freely about our successes and then to identify those things that were not working quite right, yet. Most importantly, an environment was created that allowed us to listen to one another."*
> **Doug Howard, President and CEO, Drama Kids International, Ellicott City, MD**

> *"Flo Schell's presentation was research-based, relevant, and dynamic! Her motivational style is contagious!"*
> **Judi Hughes, Provost and Peggy Kearney, Director of Education, ECPI College of Technology, Manassas, VA**

To learn more about one-day events, email Flo at: **mycoach@FloSchell.com**

Franchise Sales Professionals also are invited to experience the power of Individual Franchise Coaching. You choose the goals… we co-create the actions! Here's a testimonial from another client:

> "In three months, I changed from someone who felt uncomfortable with my positions, responsibilities, and some of my working relationships. Now I know exactly what to do and how I should do it if I want to be successful. I feel more confident. Her coaching was tactful, inspirational, and honest."
> **Tanya Mitchell, VP Franchise Development,
> Learning Rx, Colorado**

To learn more at no obligation, email the author at:

mycoach@FloSchell.com

If you are a sales professional who is seeking to add the evolutionary principles of coaching to your sales approach, you are invited to take a look at the following:

www.TerriLevine.com/coaching-selling.html

There you will find an 8-session Audio CD Series entitled, *Coaching and Selling: Perfect Together*. This series is co-sponsored by Franchise Coaching Systems and Comprehensive Coaching U, Inc. Your Sales Coach is Flo Schell. It's a great way to get further information through self-learning.

And available for a short while, a 3-CD Sales Success Series featuring Flo Schell live! Topics:

- Motivation… Even on the Toughest of Days
- Selling and Coaching… Perfect Together
- Closing End-of-Year Deals

To order, visit: www.FranchiseCoachingSystems.com and click on the building on the franchise coaching page. An email box will pop up and you may send your query. CDs are $19.99 each, plus shipping and handling.

Mention you are a book reader and receive your $24.95 discount on the full package, only while supplies last.

To stay in touch for future offerings and state-of-the-art sales programs, please stay connected through the author's free quarterly newsletter, *The Future of Franchising*. For free registration, visit **www.FranchiseCoachingSystems.com.**

If you are a franchise company and need help with writing or updating your Operations Manual, you will get outstanding service from Valerie Maione at Mid-Atlantic Franchise Associates; 410-964-1884, or vmaione@comcast.net.

If you are an owner of a franchised business or are seeking to buy a franchised business, you are invited to visit www.franchisegator.com for up-to-date articles of interest and franchise-related resources.

To stay current on topics related to franchising, consider a subscription to *Franchise Update Magazine* **www.franchise-update.com** and *Franchise Times Magazine* **www.franchisetimes.com.** Both are industry favorites.

ARE YOU A LEADER AND EAGER TO LIVE YOUR BEST LIFE? TRY THESE RESPECTED RESOURCES:

If you're anything like me, you know that leaders have lives at home as well as at work. Wouldn't you like to have every resource available for self-growth, too, so that you can be your best self in both arenas?

In my experiences as a Coach, a Sales Professional, and a Business Owner, I know that personalities can have a huge effect on our success. When the personalities of the people in our offices and businesses are compatible, we thrive. When those same personalities get in the way, we don't. Wouldn't it be great to quickly understand the personality types of your managers, colleagues, and customers?

For those of you interested in this subject, I recommend the work of Dr. Carol Ritberger. Her book, *What Color is Your Personality?*, has been an inspiration to me and is simply lots of fun to read. Take her Personality Profile at **www.Ritberger.com** to find out your color today! And if you're a Yellow, let me know!

Interested in taking your business to the million-dollar level? I can't think of a better person to contact than Andrea J. Lee at **www.AndreaJLee.com**. Andrea is internationally known for her huge mind and loving approach to extreme business growth. I just don't know anyone better!

Curious about how Relationship Coaching can enhance your life or the lives of your loved ones? Visit Lisa Kramer, a great relationship coach and respected mentor at **www.LivingwithIntention.com** and **www.LovingwithIntention.com**. She is sure to treat you with good care.

Just want to stay in touch? Please do so in any way that is comfortable for you. Flo can be reached at: **mycoach@FloSchell.com**.

Ciao for now… but not for long!

Flo Schell

About the Author

Flo Schell is a Personal and Business Coach who helps small-business owners boost their confidence and sell with ease. Her love of sales shines through as she supports individuals and companies in their growth. As former Vice President of Franchise Development for Sylvan Learning Systems, Inc., she and her sales team more than doubled the number of units in the system from 300 to 750+. In that role, Flo was awarded the distinction of "Franchise Super Salesperson of the Year" in *Franchise Update* magazine.

Today she combines those selling skills with evolutionary coaching skills, helping small-business owners everywhere build their businesses with integrity and comfort.

And, her reputation for helping sales professionals to excel is international in scope!

As a Sales Coach, Flo may be best known for her work with innovative franchise companies and their people. Her clients include: International Center for Entrepreneurial Development, Drama Kids International, Carpet Network, Huntington Learning Centers, and more.

Franchise Coaching Systems publishes "The Future of Franchising" newsletter quarterly. Free registration is available at: www.FranchiseCoachingSystems.com

"Thanks, Flo! I like how you mesh instinct with practicality."
—**Sandy Krzyzanowski, Franchise Times**

Flo treasures her work with her personal coaching clients, too. Her distinction as a Certified Coach provides her clients with state-of-the-art coaching techniques. She uses a heart-based approach to help clients get to the core of things quickly and effectively. To stay connected, register for her free newsletter, "Just go with the Flow": www.FloSchell.com.

"It is evident that Flo comes from a special place in her coaching… her heart!"
—**Carlisa Bryant, Boone, NC**

Printed in the United States
68784LVS00002B/1-99